FRACTAL FACE

BY
OBADIAH MICHAEL CREEK

ISBN:9798378588459

"KNOW THYSELF." --SOCRATES

FRACTAL FACE

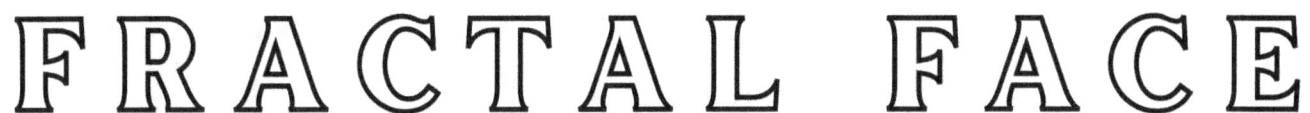

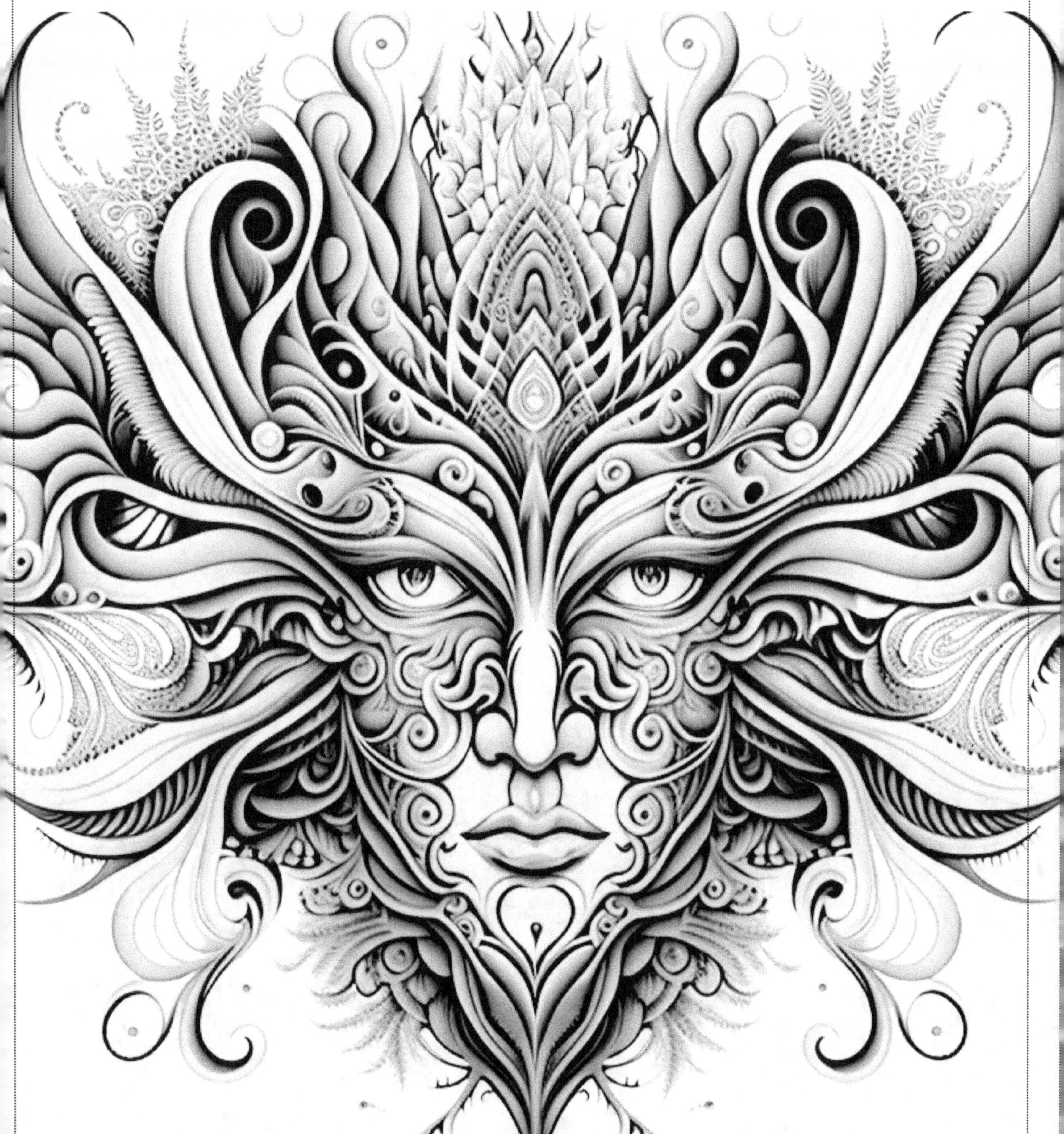

**"THE JOURNEY OF A THOUSAND MILES
BEGINS WITH ONE STEP" --LAO TZU**

FRACTAL FACE

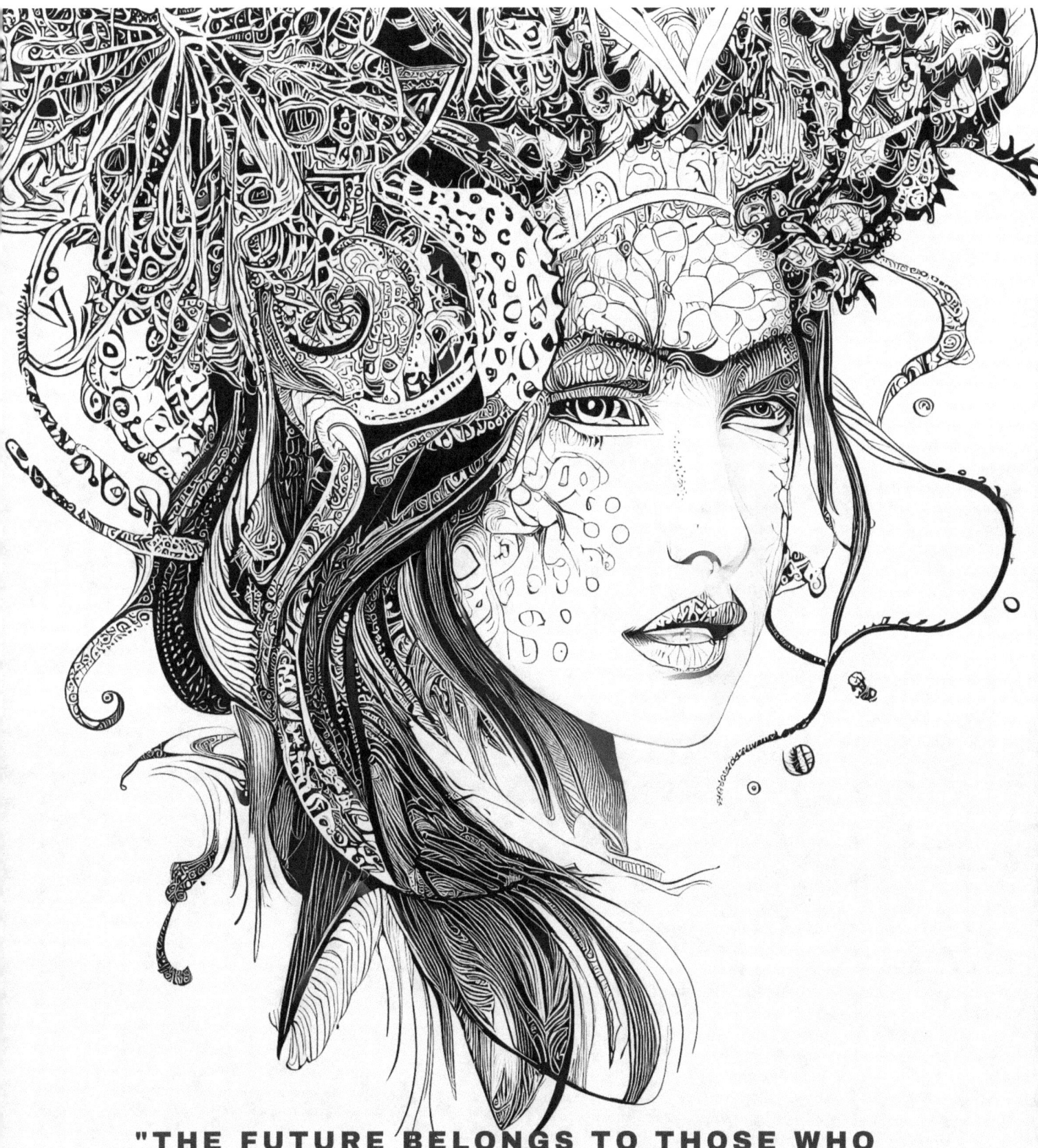

"THE FUTURE BELONGS TO THOSE WHO BELIEVE IN THE BEAUTY OF THEIR DREAMS" -- ELEANOR ROOSEVELT

FRACTAL FACE

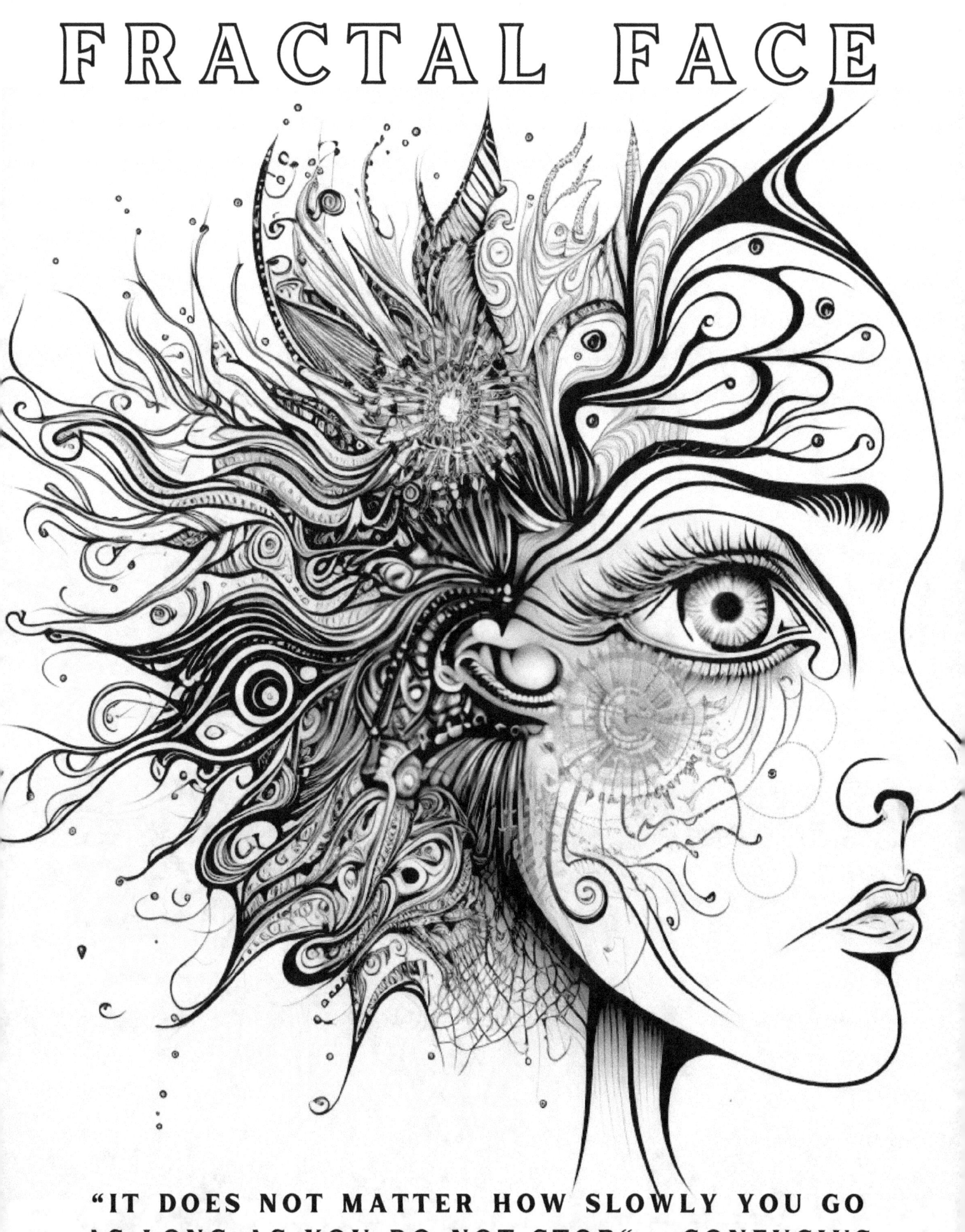

"IT DOES NOT MATTER HOW SLOWLY YOU GO
AS LONG AS YOU DO NOT STOP" --CONFUCIUS

FRACTAL FACE

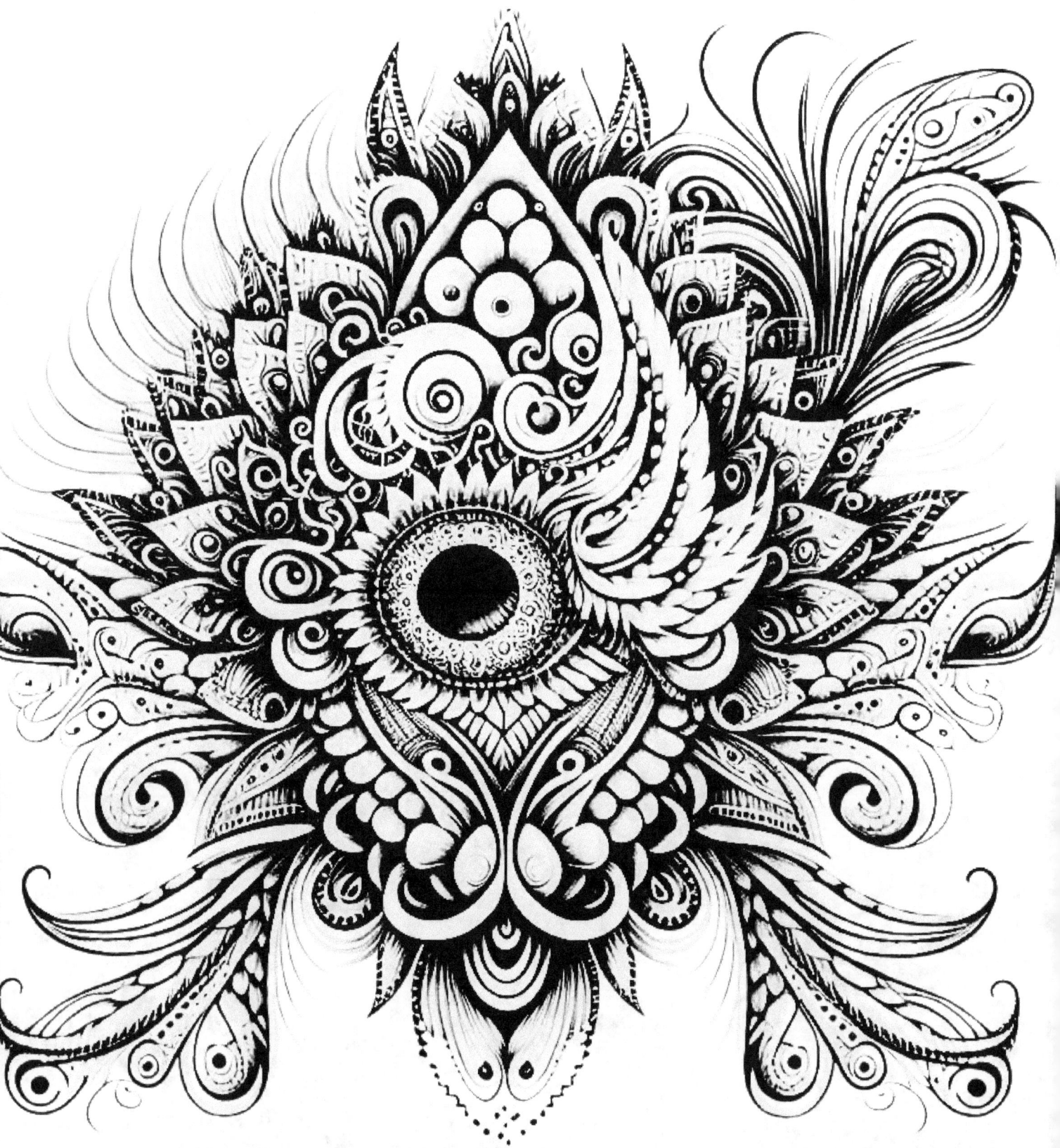

"BE THE CHANGE YOU WISH TO SEE IN THE WORLD"   --MAHATMA GANDHI

HEAVENLY BODIES

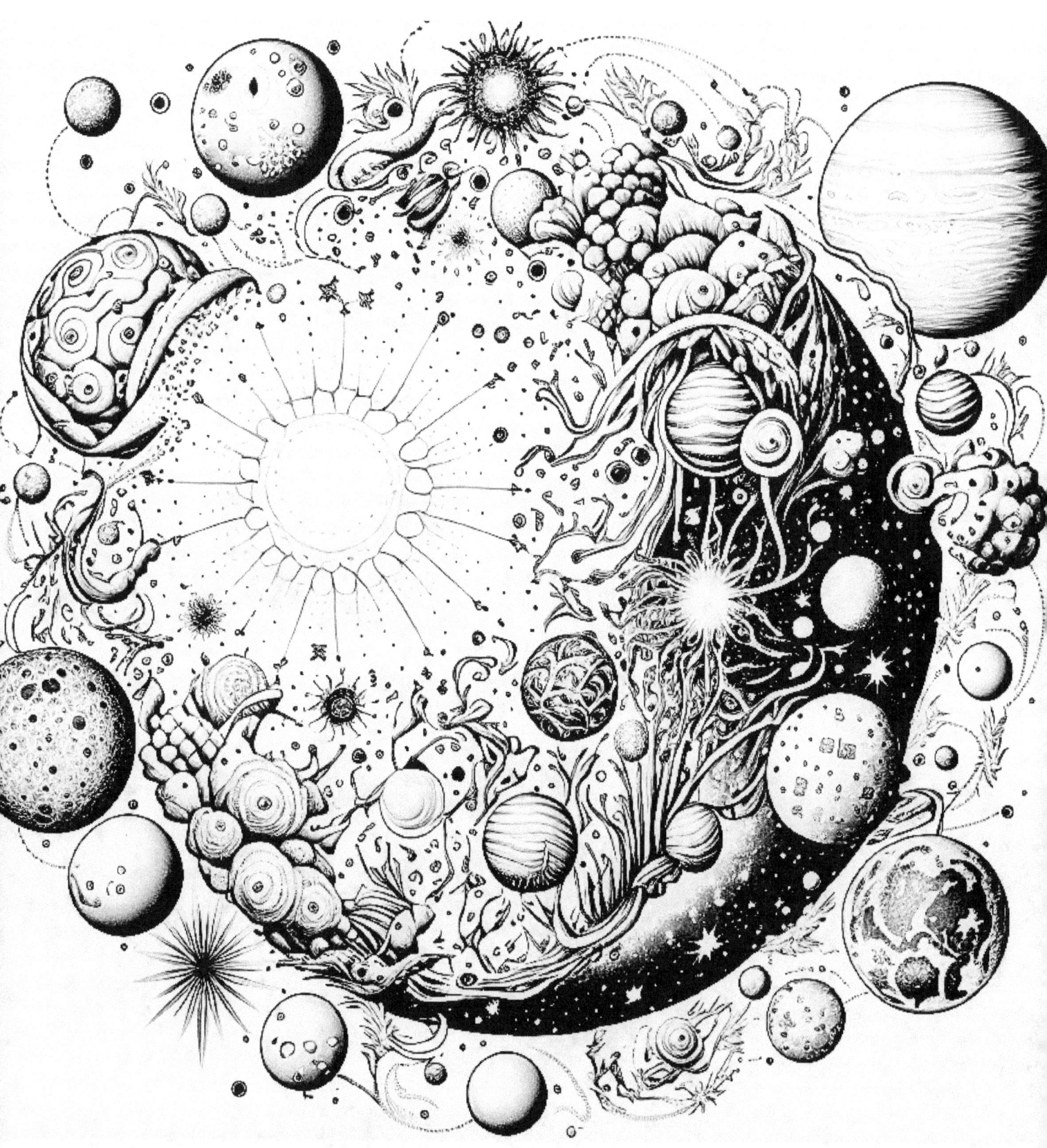

"THE BEST WAY TO PREDICT THE FUTURE IS TO CREATE IT" --ABRAHAM LINCOLN

HEAVENLY BODIES

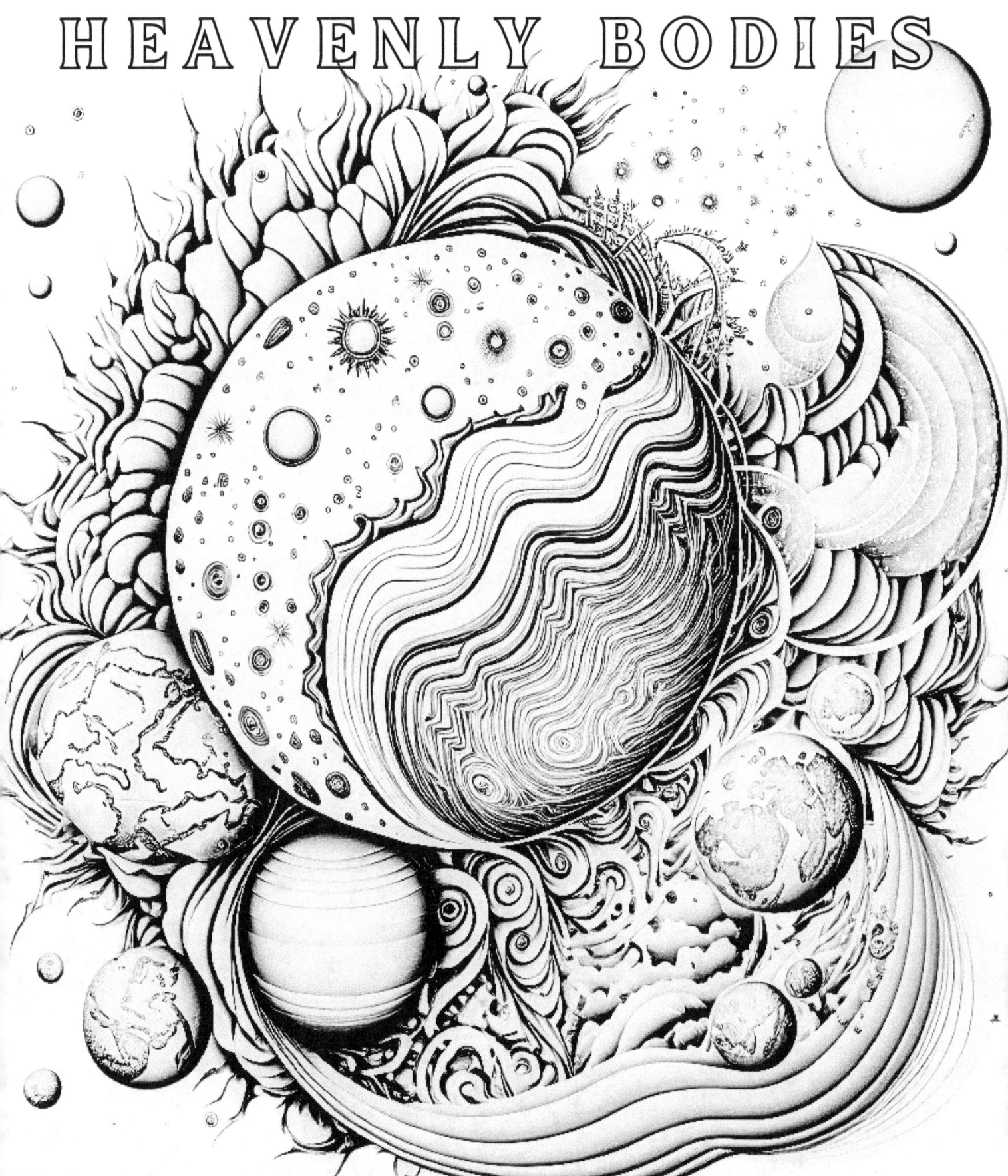

"THE ONLY PERSON YOU ARE DESTINED TO BECOME
IS THE PERSON YOU DECIDE TO BE" --RALPH
WALDO EMERSON

HEAVENLY BODIES

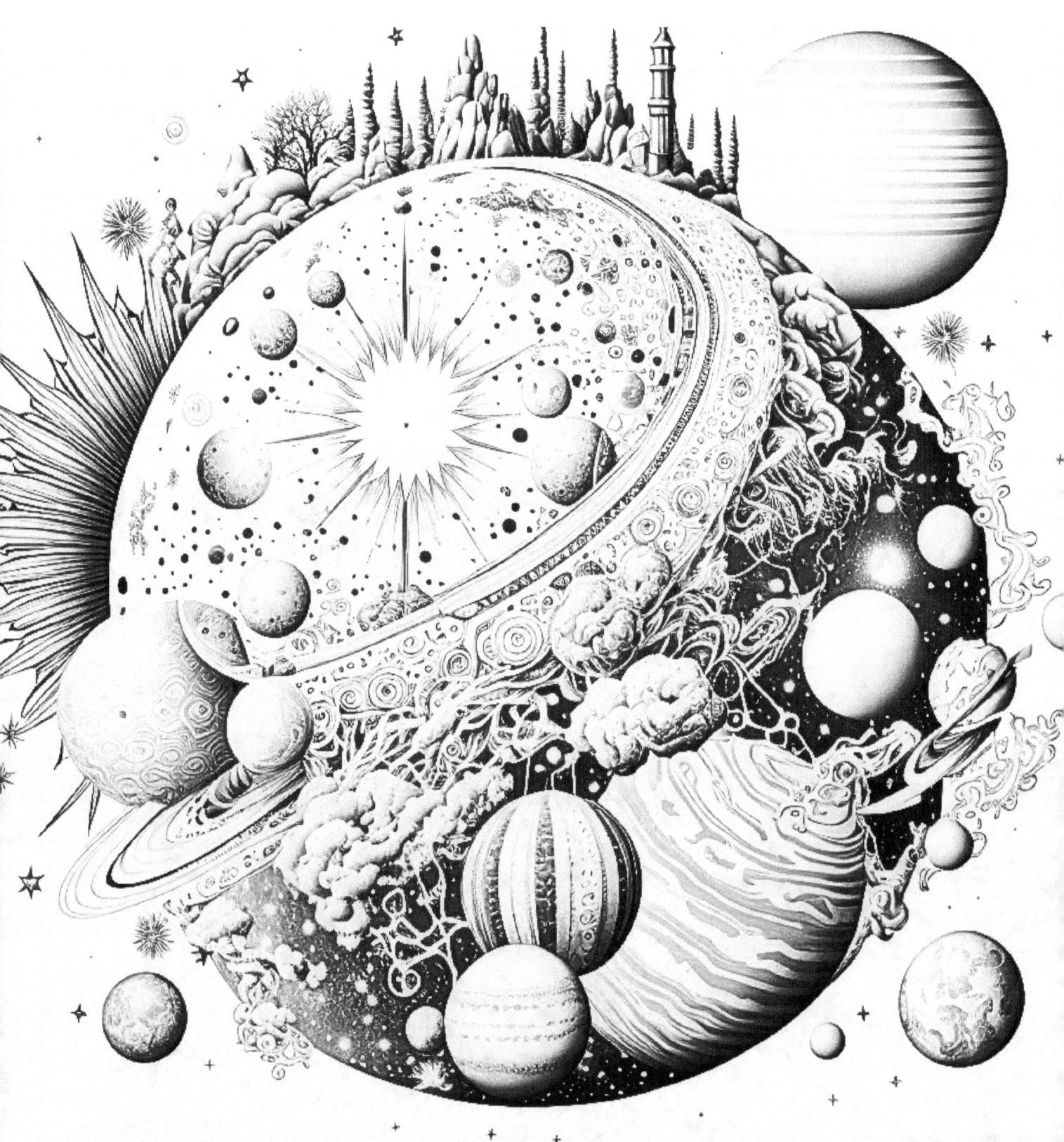

"IF YOU CANNOT DO GREAT THINGS, DO SMALL THINGS IN A GREAT WAY" --NAPOLEON HILL

HEAVENLY BODIES

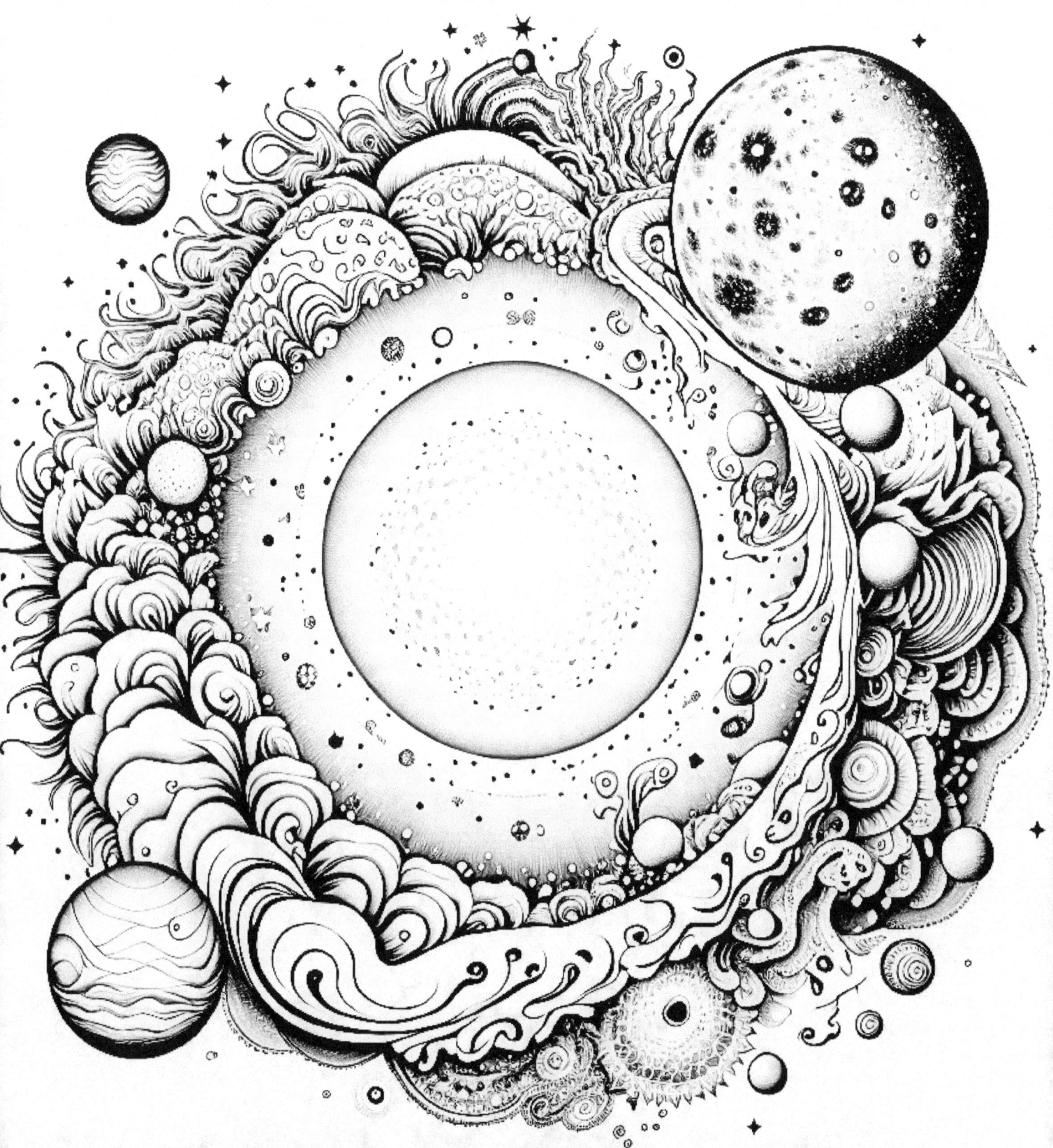

"LIFE ISN'T ABOUT FINDING YOURSELF. LIFE IS ABOUT CREATING YOURSELF" --GEORGE BERNARD SHAW

HEAVENLY BODIES

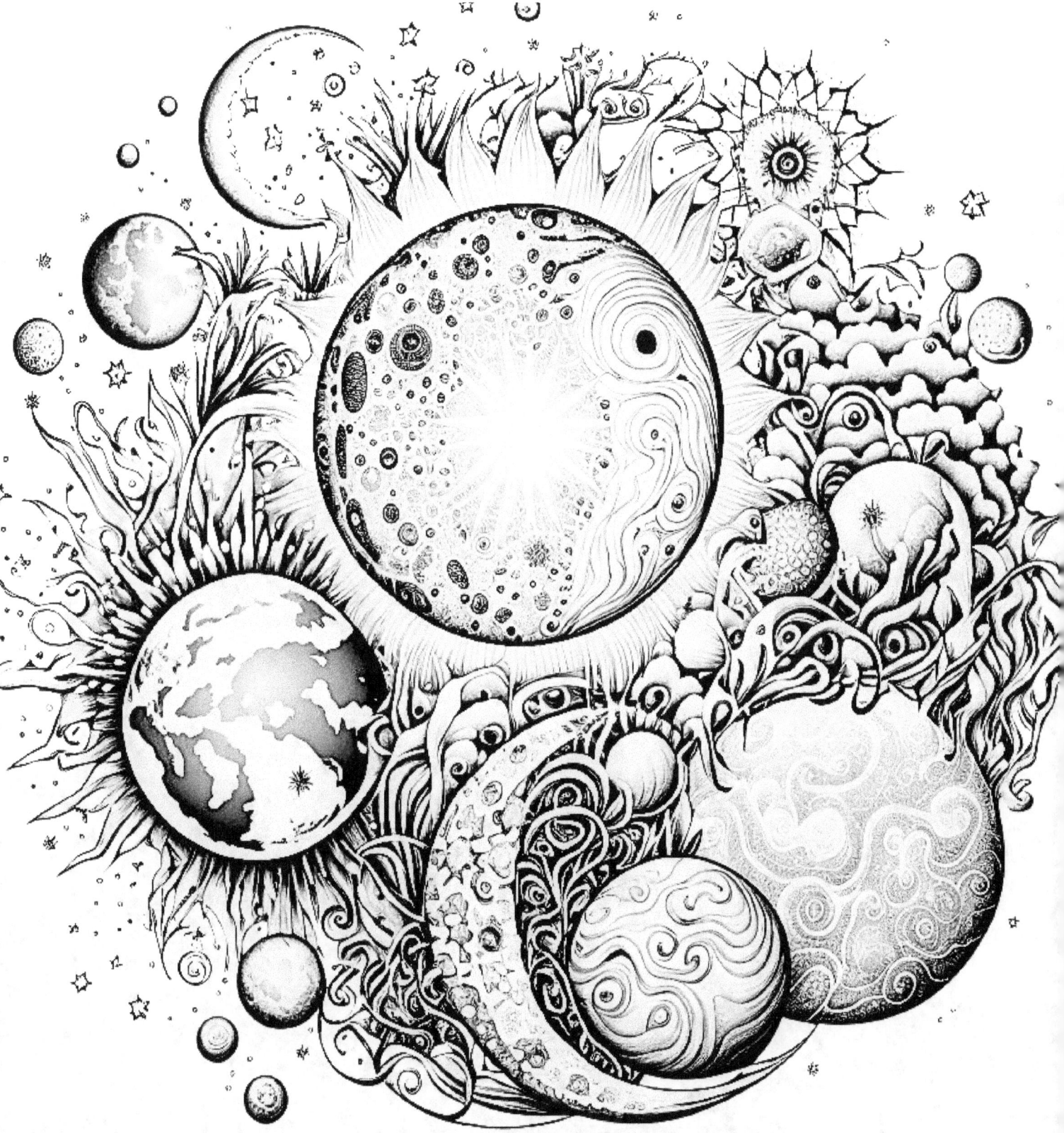

"LIFE IS NOT A PROBLEM TO BE SOLVED, BUT A REALITY TO BE EXPERIENCED" --SOREN KIERKEGAARD

HEAVENLY BODIES

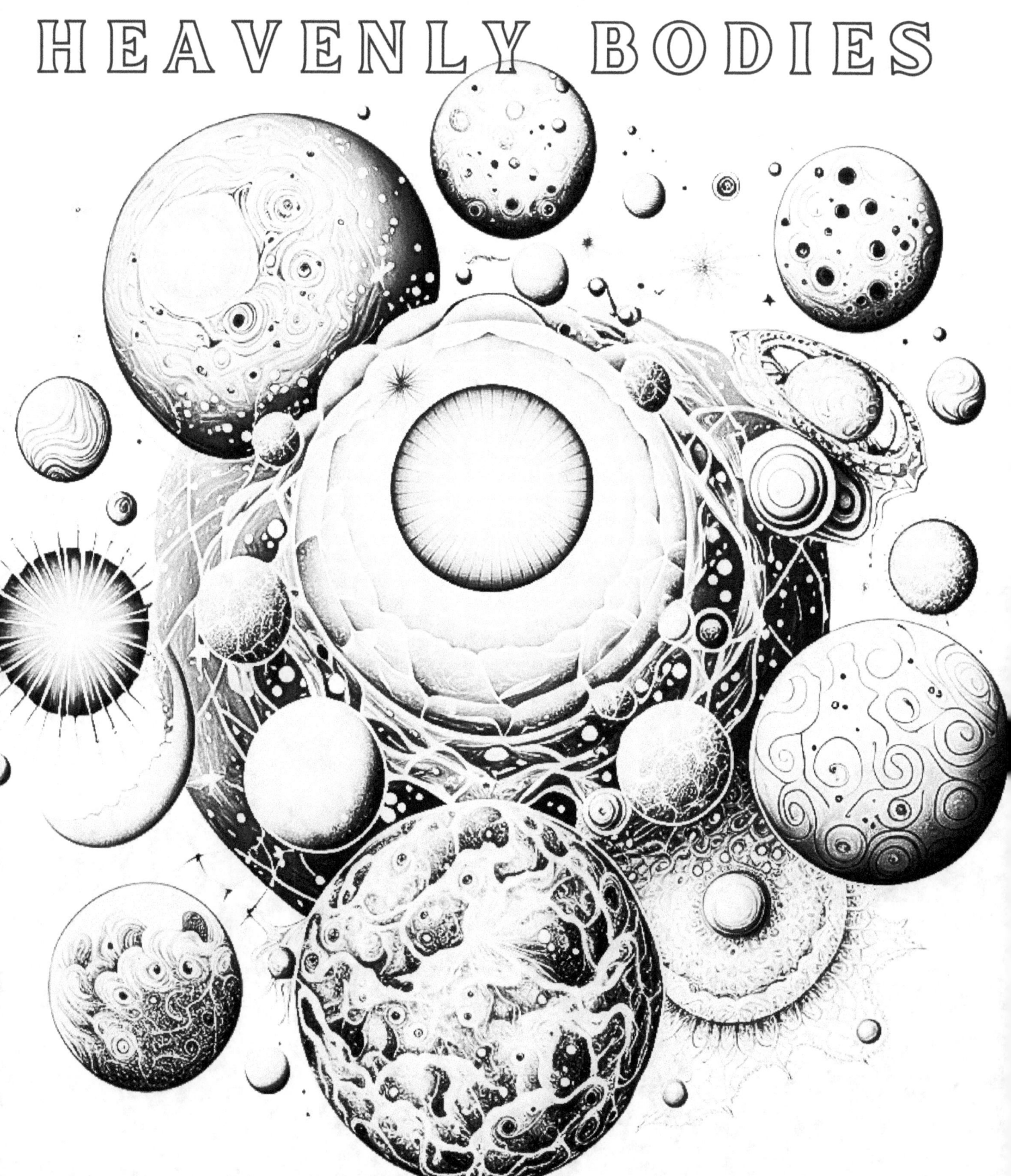

"LIFE IS WHAT HAPPENS WHEN YOU'RE BUSY MAKING OTHER PLANS" --JOHN LENNON

STRANGE ATTRACTORS

STRANGE ATTRACTORS ARE FASCINATING MATHEMATICAL OBJECTS THAT ARISE IN THE STUDY OF CHAOS THEORY AND NONLINEAR DYNAMICS. THEY ARE CALLED "STRANGE" BECAUSE OF THEIR COMPLEX, ERRATIC BEHAVIOR, AND "ATTRACTORS" BECAUSE THEY DRAW NEARBY POINTS IN PHASE SPACE TOWARDS THEM, AS IF THEY WERE MAGNETIC.

TO UNDERSTAND STRANGE ATTRACTORS, IMAGINE A SYSTEM OF EQUATIONS THAT DESCRIBES THE BEHAVIOR OF A PHYSICAL SYSTEM, SUCH AS A PENDULUM OR A WEATHER PATTERN

IN SUCH A SYSTEM, A STRANGE ATTRACTOR IS A SET OF POINTS IN PHASE SPACE THAT THE SYSTEM TENDS TO APPROACH OVER TIME, DESPITE ITS CHAOTIC BEHAVIOR. THESE POINTS CAN FORM INTRICATE, FRACTAL-LIKE PATTERNS THAT NEVER REPEAT THEMSELVES EXACTLY, EVEN THOUGH THEY ARE ATTRACTED TO THE SAME REGION OF PHASE SPACE. JUST AS A STRANGE ATTRACTOR DRAWS NEARBY POINTS IN PHASE SPACE TOWARDS IT, A BOOK ABOUT FRACTALS CAN DRAW THE ATTENTION AND INTEREST OF A PERSON WHO IS CURIOUS ABOUT THESE FASCINATING MATHEMATICAL OBJECTS. THE MORE THE PERSON LEARNS ABOUT FRACTALS, THE MORE THEY MAY BE DRAWN TOWARDS THE SUBJECT, JUST AS NEARBY POINTS IN PHASE SPACE ARE DRAWN TOWARDS A STRANGE ATTRACTOR.

MOREOVER, JUST AS A STRANGE ATTRACTOR CAN EXHIBIT BEAUTY AND COMPLEXITY, SO TOO CAN THE STUDY OF FRACTALS. THE PATTERNS AND STRUCTURES THAT EMERGE FROM THIS STUDY CAN BE BOTH SURPRISING AND AESTHETICALLY PLEASING, AND CAN INSPIRE CREATIVITY AND INNOVATION IN FIELDS RANGING FROM ART TO SCIENCE TO TECHNOLOGY.

THE CONCEPT OF STRANGE ATTRACTORS IS A FASCINATING EXAMPLE OF HOW COMPLEX AND UNPREDICTABLE BEHAVIOR CAN ARISE FROM SIMPLE MATHEMATICAL EQUATIONS. AND JUST AS A STRANGE ATTRACTOR CAN DRAW NEARBY POINTS IN PHASE SPACE TOWARDS IT, SO TOO CAN A BOOK ABOUT FRACTALS DRAW THE INTEREST AND CURIOSITY OF A PERSON, LEADING THEM DOWN A PATH OF DISCOVERY AND APPRECIATION FOR THE BEAUTY AND COMPLEXITY OF THE WORLD AROUND US.

STRANGE ATTRACTORS

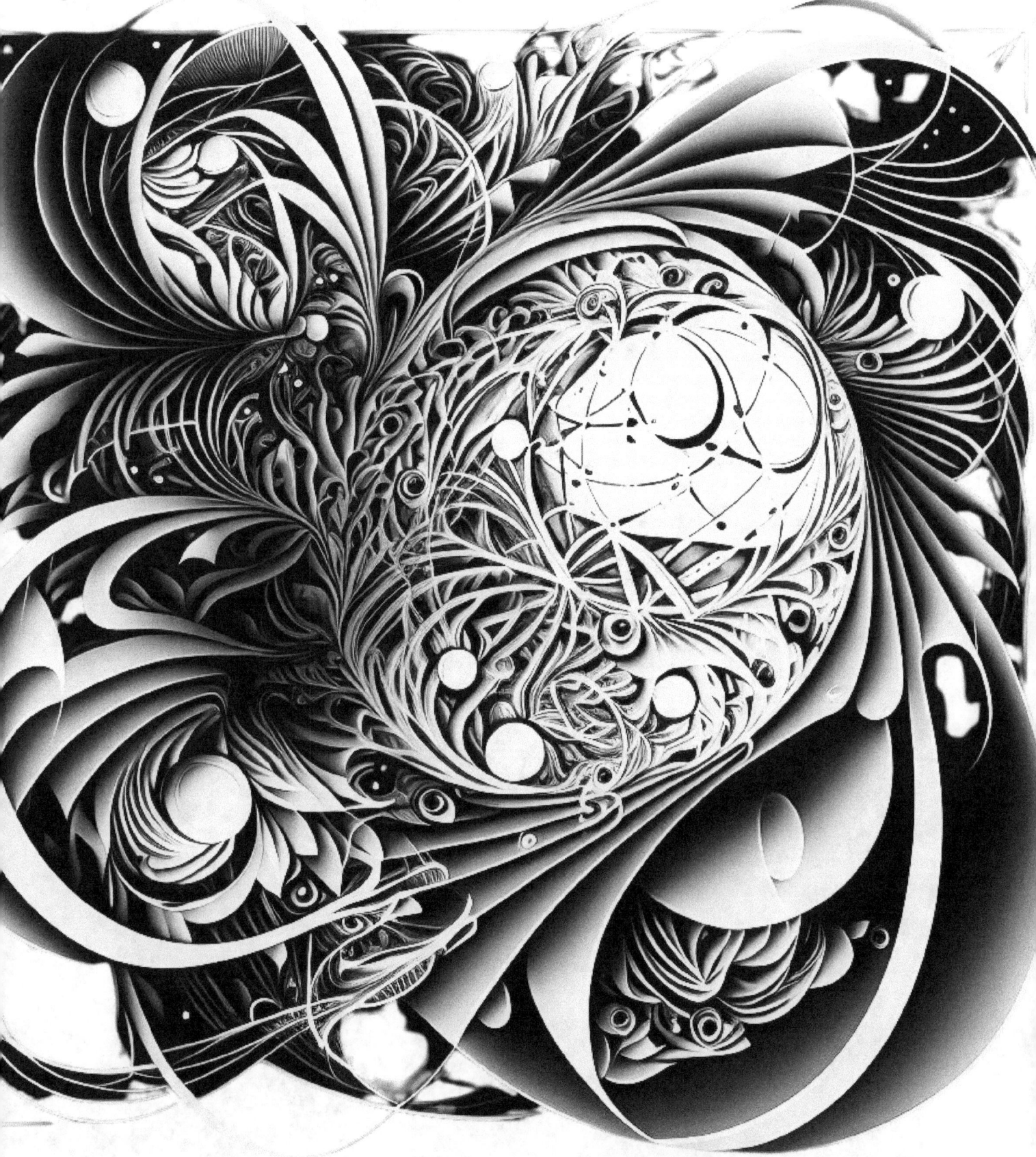

"IF YOU WANT TO LIFT YOURSELF UP, LIFT UP SOMEONE ELSE"
--BOOKER T. WASHINGTON

STRANGE ATTRACTORS

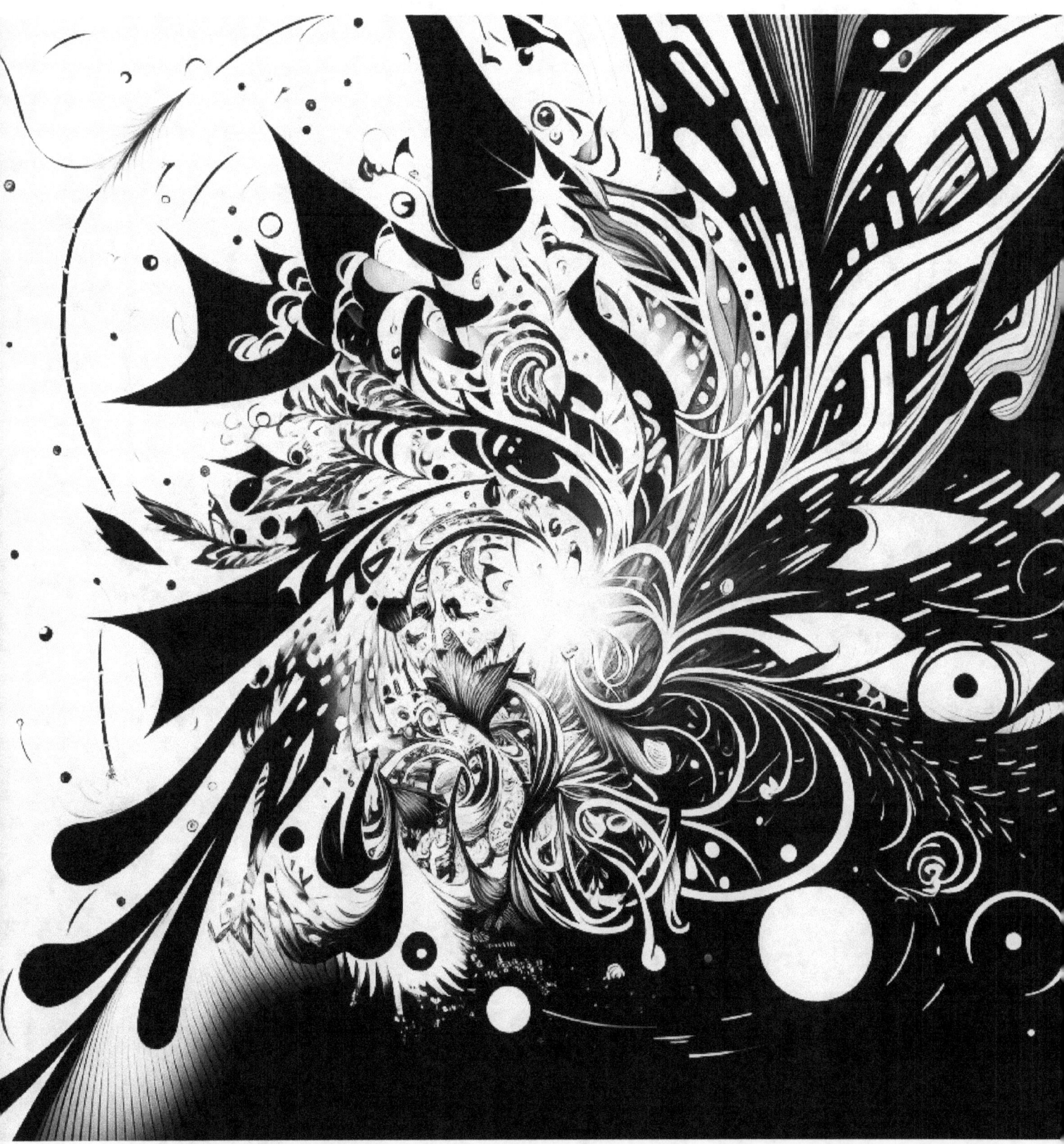

"LIFE IS NOT ABOUT WAITING FOR THE STORM TO PASS, IT'S ABOUT LEARNING TO DANCE IN THE RAIN" --VIVIAN GREENE

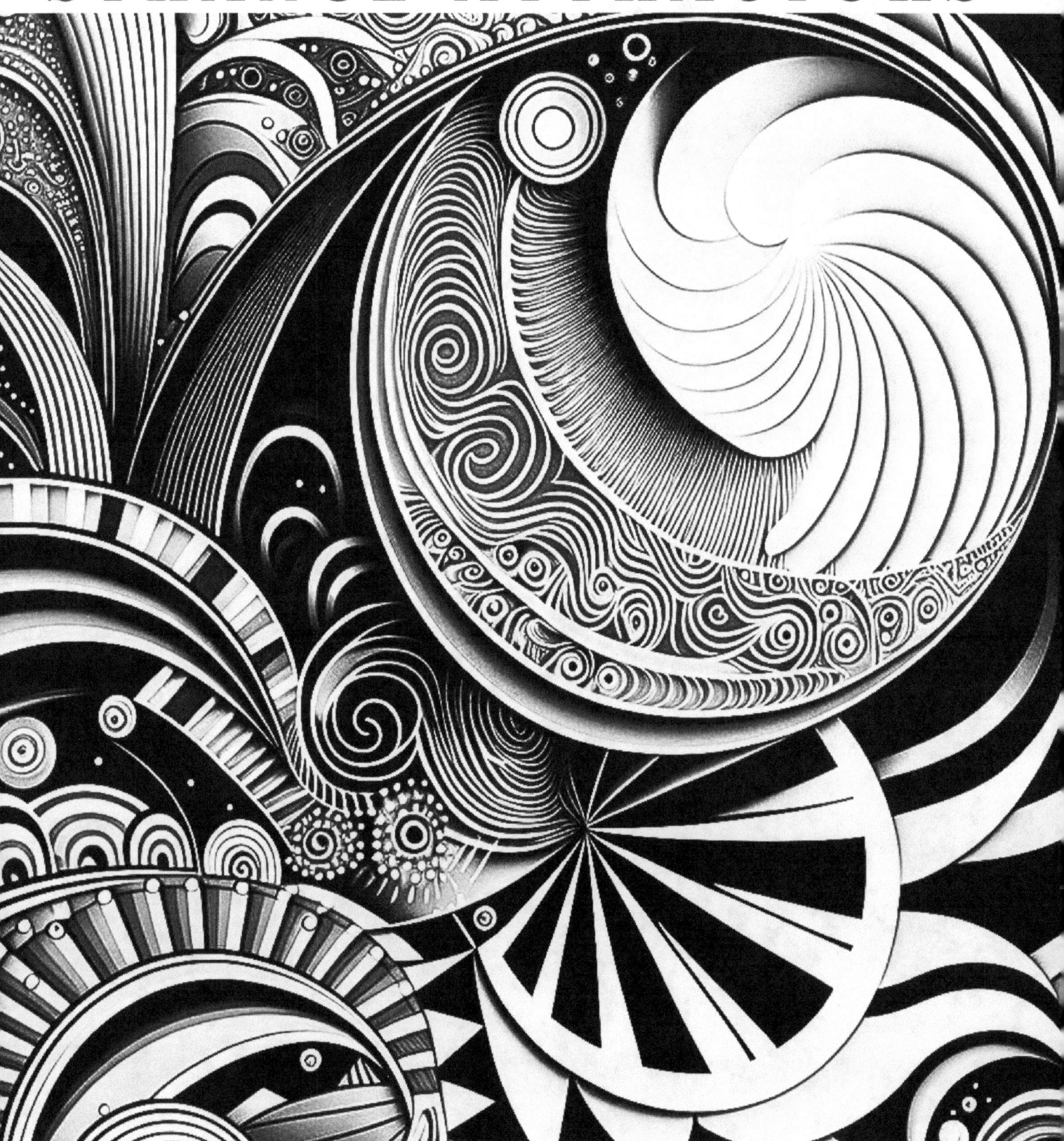

"DON'T JUDGE EACH DAY BY THE HARVEST YOU REAP BUT BY THE SEEDS
THAT YOU PLANT" --ROBERT LOUIS STEVENSON

STRANGE ATTRACTORS

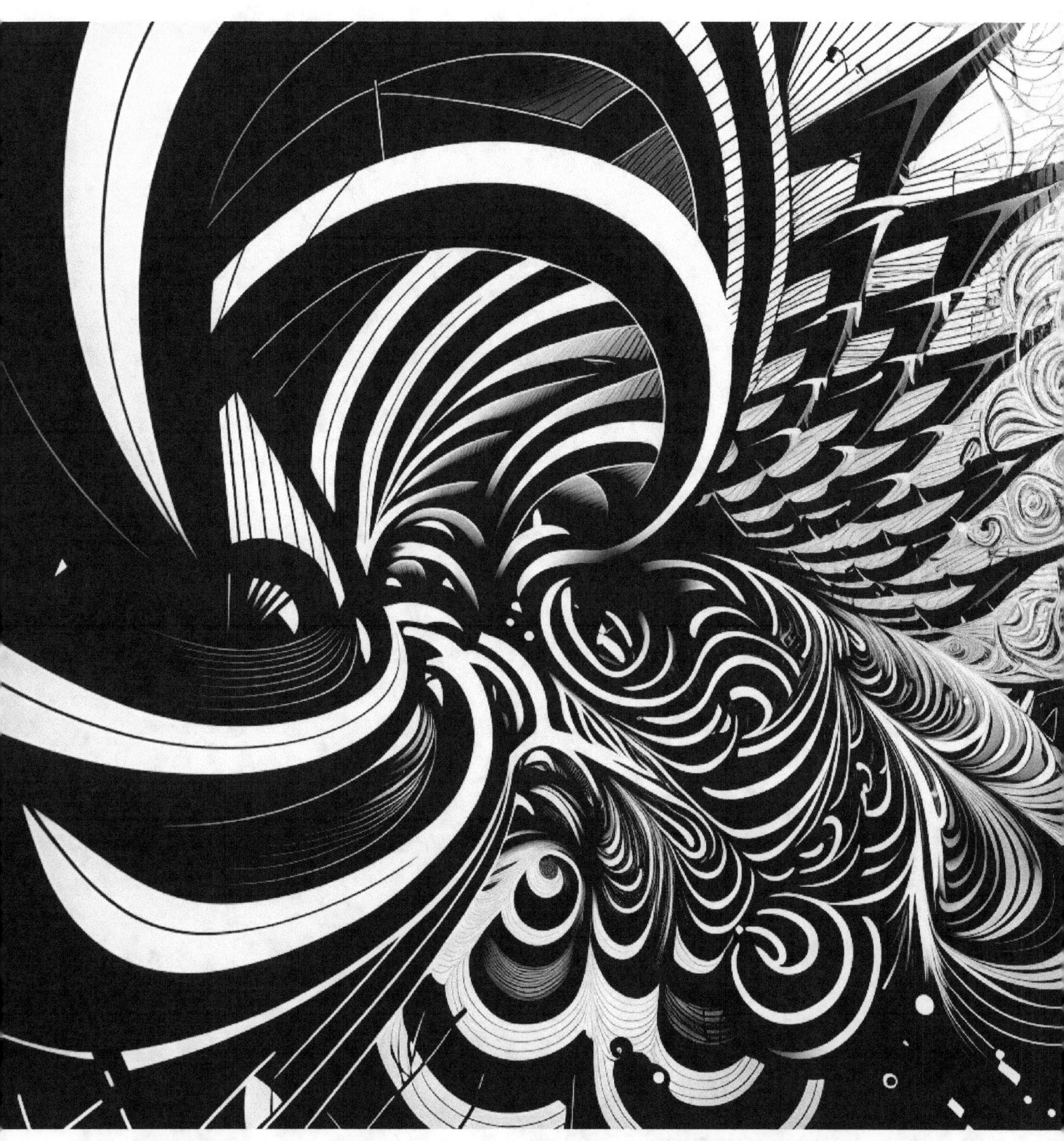

"CHANGE WILL NOT COME IF WE WAIT FOR SOME OTHER PERSON OR SOME OTHER TIME. WE ARE THE ONES WE'VE BEEN WAITING FOR. WE ARE THE CHANGE THAT WE SEEK." --BARACK OBAMA

FRACTAL MEGOPOLIS

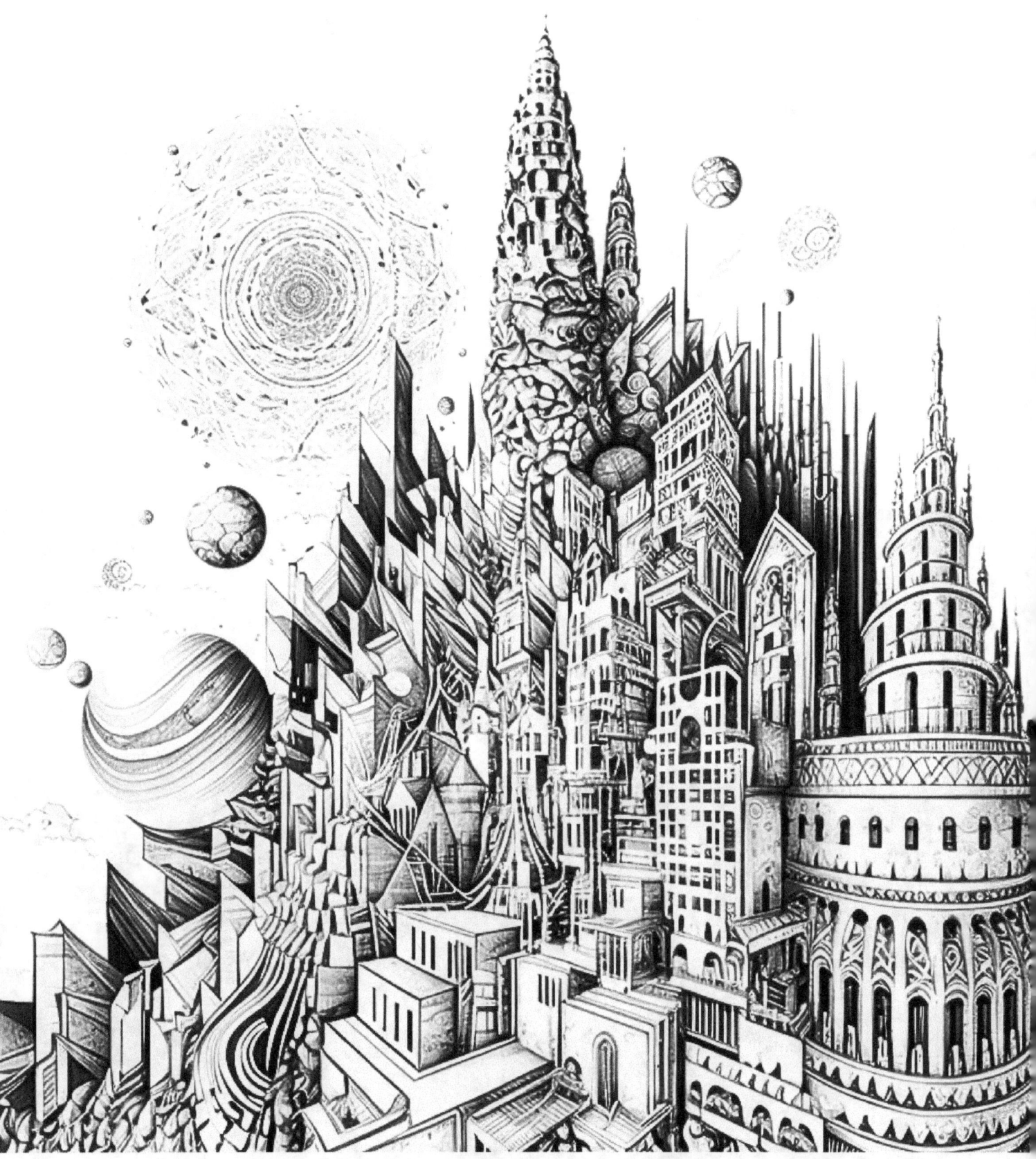

"TELL ME AND I FORGET. TEACH ME AND I REMEMBER. INVOLVE ME AND I LEARN" --BENJAMIN FRANKLIN

FRACTAL MEGOPOLIS

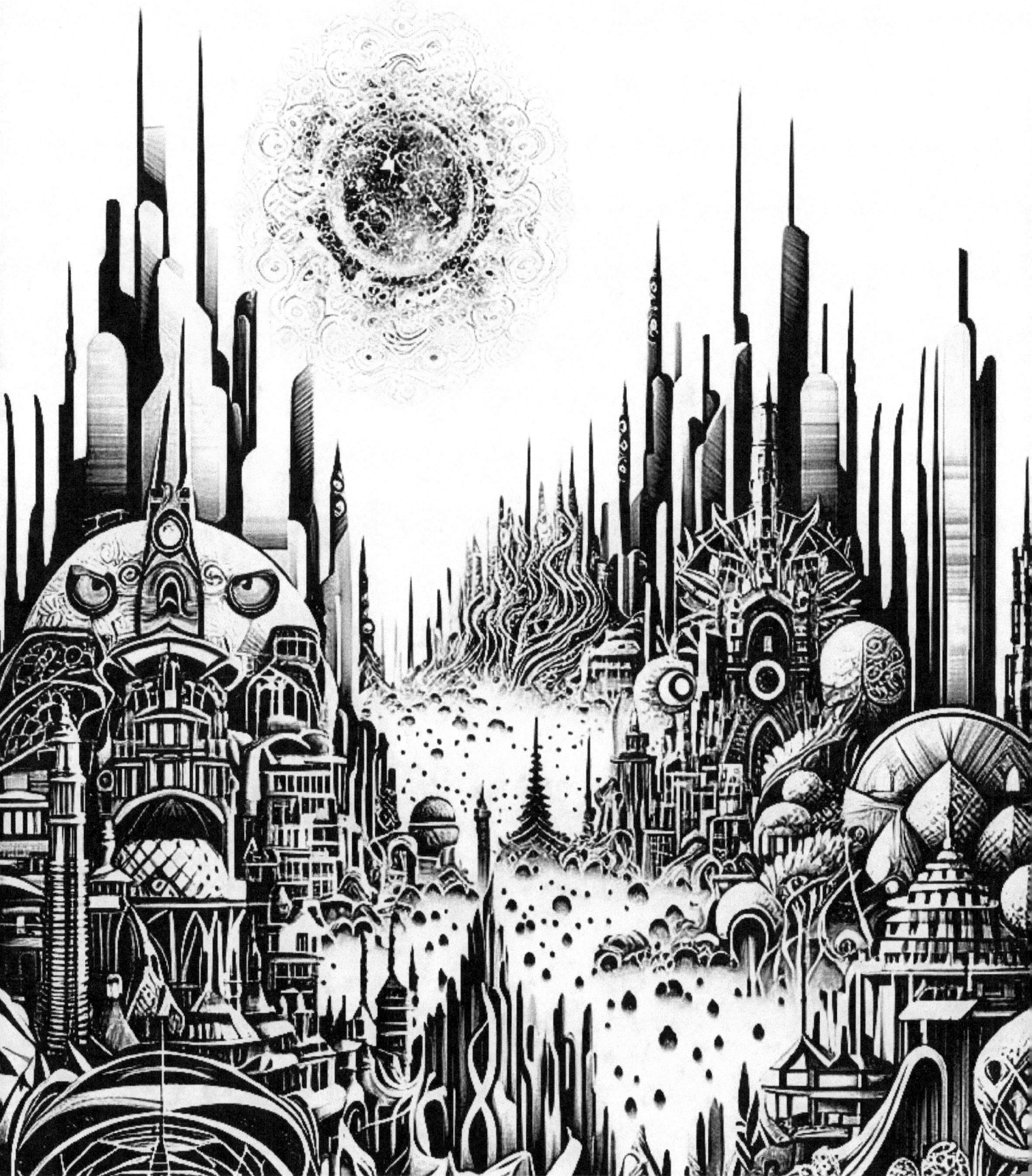

"THE ONLY WAY TO HAVE A FRIEND IS TO BE ONE"
--RALPH WALDO EMERSON

FRACTAL MEGOPOLIS

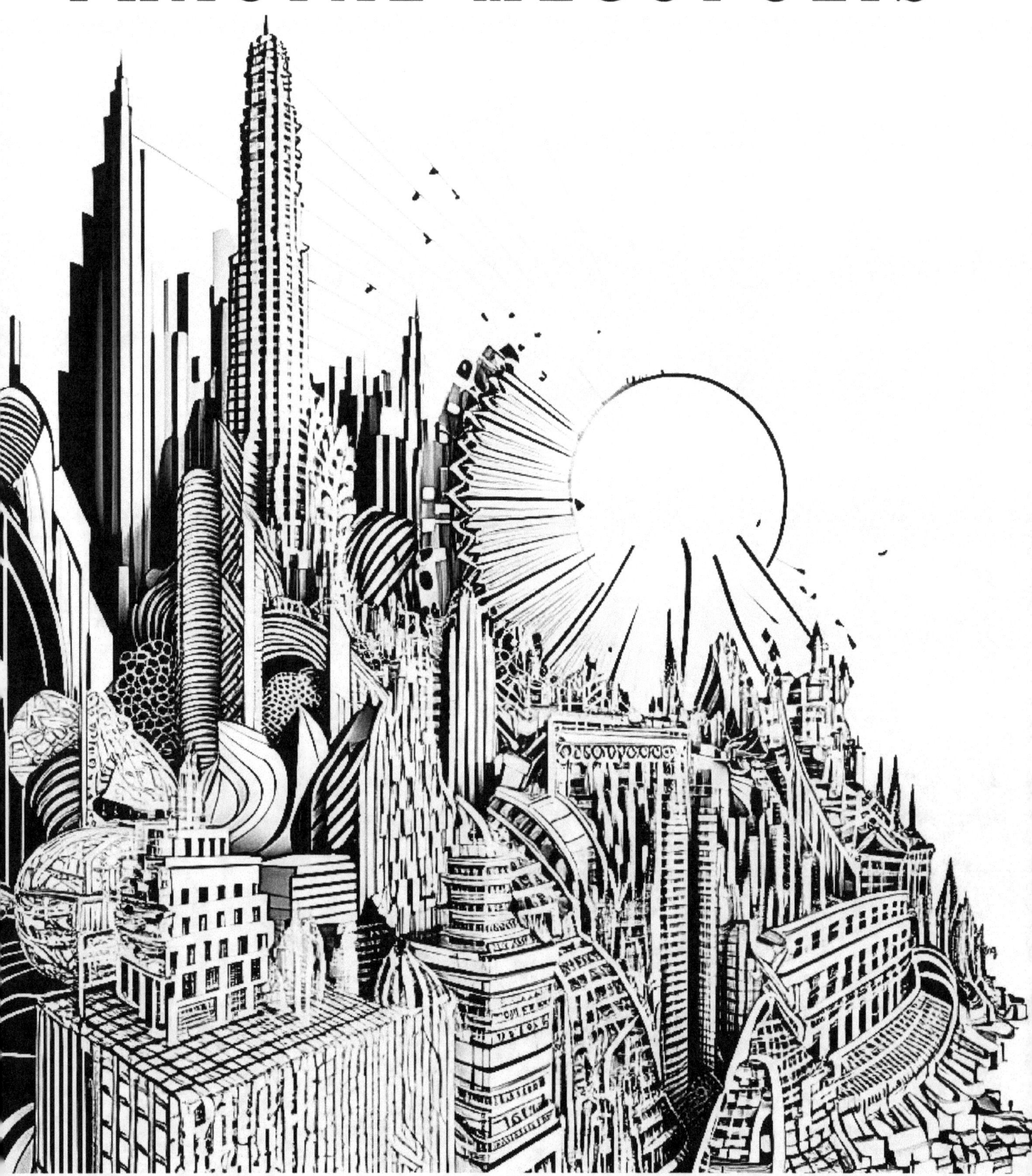

"ACTIONS SPEAK LOUDER THAN WORDS"
--ABRAHAM LINCOLN

FRACTAL MINDS

FRACTALS, CHAOS THEORY, AND COMPLEXITY THEORY ARE FASCINATING CONCEPTS THAT OFFER INSIGHT INTO THE WAY OUR WORLD WORKS. AT FIRST GLANCE, THEY MAY APPEAR TO BE ABSTRACT MATHEMATICAL CONCEPTS, BUT THEY HAVE PROFOUND PHILOSOPHICAL IMPLICATIONS THAT CAN HELP US BETTER UNDERSTAND OUR PLACE IN THE WORLD AND THE INTERCONNECTEDNESS OF ALL THINGS.

ONE WAY TO UNDERSTAND THE CONCEPT OF EMERGENT ORDER IS TO CONSIDER THE BEHAVIOR OF A FLOCK OF BIRDS. WHEN VIEWED INDIVIDUALLY, THE BIRDS' BEHAVIOR SEEMS CHAOTIC AND UNPREDICTABLE. BUT WHEN VIEWED AS A WHOLE, THEIR BEHAVIOR CREATES A BEAUTIFUL, ORDERED PATTERN THAT IS KNOWN AS A MURMURATION.

A MURMURATION IS A STUNNING DISPLAY OF ORDER EMERGING FROM CHAOS. THE BIRDS MOVE IN A COORDINATED MANNER, CREATING INTRICATE PATTERNS THAT SEEM ALMOST CHOREOGRAPHED. THIS EMERGENT ORDER ARISES FROM THE MANY SMALL RELATIONS BETWEEN INDIVIDUAL BIRDS, EACH RESPONDING TO THE MOVEMENTS OF THEIR NEIGHBORS.

THE SAME PRINCIPLE APPLIES TO THE HUMAN BRAIN, WHICH IS MADE UP OF BILLIONS OF INDIVIDUAL NEURONS, EACH CONNECTING TO OTHER NEURONS THROUGH A VAST NETWORK OF SYNAPSES. WHEN VIEWED INDIVIDUALLY, THESE NEURONS SEEM TO BEHAVE IN A CHAOTIC AND UNPREDICTABLE MANNER. BUT WHEN VIEWED AS A WHOLE, THEY CREATE THE COMPLEX AND ORDERED PATTERN OF OUR THOUGHTS AND CONSCIOUSNESS.

THE EMERGENT ORDER OF THE BRAIN IS A RESULT OF THE MANY SMALL RELATIONS BETWEEN INDIVIDUAL NEURONS. EACH NEURON RESPONDS TO THE SIGNALS IT RECEIVES FROM ITS NEIGHBORS, AND THIS INTERACTION CREATES THE PATTERNS OF ACTIVITY THAT GIVE RISE TO OUR THOUGHTS AND CONSCIOUSNESS.

THE STUDY OF FRACTALS AND COMPLEXITY THEORY CAN HELP US UNDERSTAND THE INTERCONNECTEDNESS OF ALL

THINGS IN NATURE. FRACTALS ARE SELF-SIMILAR PATTERNS THAT REPEAT AT DIFFERENT SCALES, AND THEY CAN BE FOUND IN MANY NATURAL PHENOMENA, SUCH AS THE BRANCHING PATTERNS OF TREES AND THE CONTOURS OF COASTLINES.

COMPLEXITY THEORY EXPLORES THE BEHAVIOR OF SYSTEMS THAT ARE COMPOSED OF MANY INTERCONNECTED PARTS. THESE SYSTEMS CAN EXHIBIT EMERGENT PROPERTIES THAT CANNOT BE PREDICTED FROM THE BEHAVIOR OF INDIVIDUAL PARTS. FOR EXAMPLE, THE BEHAVIOR OF A COLONY OF ANTS CANNOT BE PREDICTED FROM THE BEHAVIOR OF INDIVIDUAL ANTS, BUT EMERGES FROM THE MANY SMALL RELATIONS BETWEEN THEM.

THE STUDY OF FRACTALS AND COMPLEXITY CAN LEAD TO A DEEPER APPRECIATION OF THE BEAUTY AND COMPLEXITY OF THE WORLD AROUND US. IT CAN ALSO INSPIRE CREATIVITY AND INNOVATION, AS WE SEEK TO UNDERSTAND AND HARNESS THE EMERGENT PROPERTIES OF COMPLEX SYSTEMS.

BUT THE STUDY OF FRACTALS AND COMPLEXITY ALSO RAISES PHILOSOPHICAL QUESTIONS ABOUT THE NATURE OF REALITY AND OUR PLACE IN THE WORLD. ARE THE PATTERNS WE SEE IN NATURE THE RESULT OF FUNDAMENTAL LAWS OF THE UNIVERSE, OR ARE THEY THE RESULT OF THE INTERACTIONS BETWEEN INDIVIDUAL PARTS? IS THERE A DEEPER ORDER TO THE UNIVERSE, OR IS IT ALL JUST EMERGENT PROPERTIES ARISING FROM THE INTERACTIONS OF MANY SMALL PARTS?

THE IDEA OF INTERCONNECTEDNESS IS ALSO CENTRAL TO THE STUDY OF FRACTALS AND COMPLEXITY. THE PATTERNS WE SEE IN NATURE ARE NOT ISOLATED PHENOMENA, BUT ARE INTERCONNECTED WITH EVERYTHING ELSE IN THE WORLD. THE SAME IS TRUE OF HUMAN SOCIETY, WHERE THE ACTIONS OF INDIVIDUALS CAN HAVE FAR-REACHING CONSEQUENCES FOR OTHERS.

THIS INTERCONNECTEDNESS HAS ETHICAL AND SOCIAL IMPLICATIONS, PARTICULARLY IN RELATION TO ISSUES SUCH AS SOCIAL JUSTICE AND ENVIRONMENTAL SUSTAINABILITY. THE STUDY OF FRACTALS AND COMPLEXITY CAN HELP US BETTER UNDERSTAND THE COMPLEX SYSTEMS THAT UNDERPIN OUR WORLD, AND CAN PROVIDE INSIGHTS INTO HOW WE CAN CREATE A MORE JUST AND SUSTAINABLE SOCIETY.

IN CONCLUSION, THE STUDY OF FRACTALS, CHAOS THEORY, AND COMPLEXITY THEORY OFFERS A PROFOUND AND FASCINATING INSIGHT INTO THE NATURE OF REALITY AND OUR PLACE IN THE WORLD. FROM THE EMERGENT ORDER OF A FLOCK OF BIRDS TO THE COMPLEXITY OF THE HUMAN BRAIN, THESE CONCEPTS CAN HELP US BETTER UNDERSTAND THE INTERCONNECTEDNESS OF ALL THINGS AND INSPIRE US TO APPRECIATE THE BEAUTY AND COMPLEXITY OF THE WORLD AROUND US.

FRACTAL MINDS

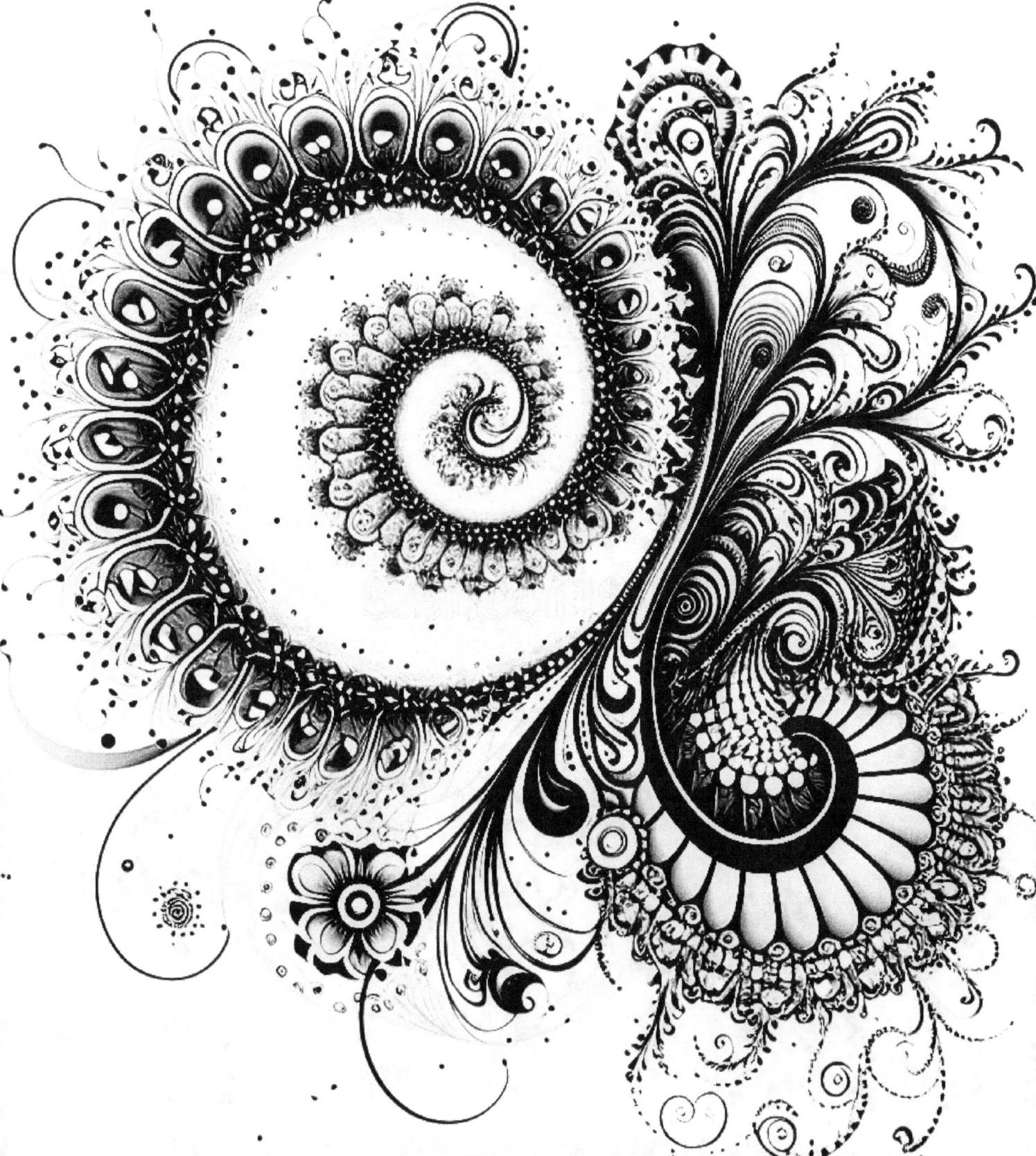

"DO NOT LET WHAT YOU CANNOT DO INTERFERE
WITH WHAT YOU CAN DO" --JOHN WOODEN

FRACTAL MINDS

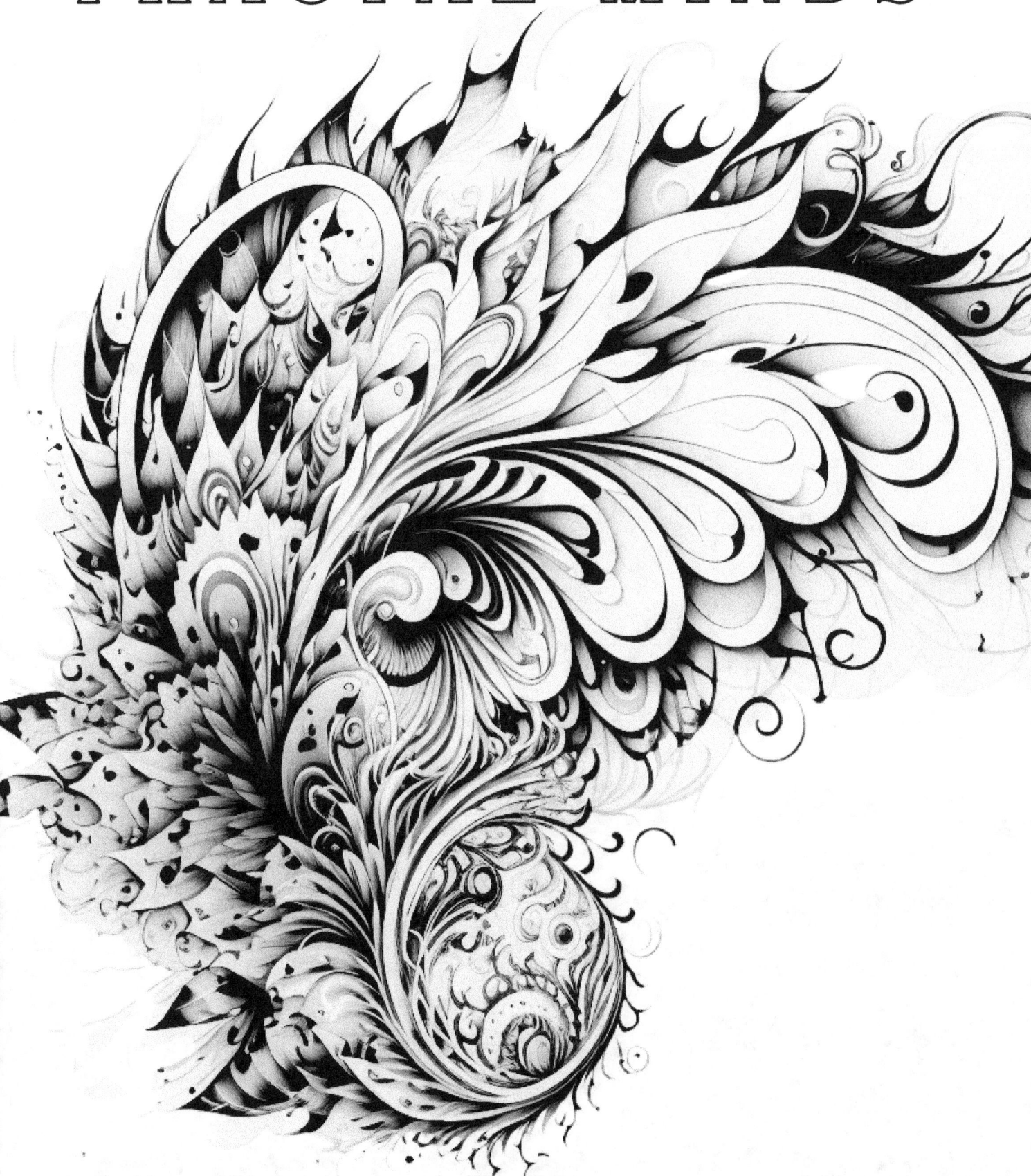

"HE WHO HAS A WHY TO LIVE CAN BEAR ALMOST ANY HOW." —FRIEDRICH NIETZSCHE

FRACTAL MINDS

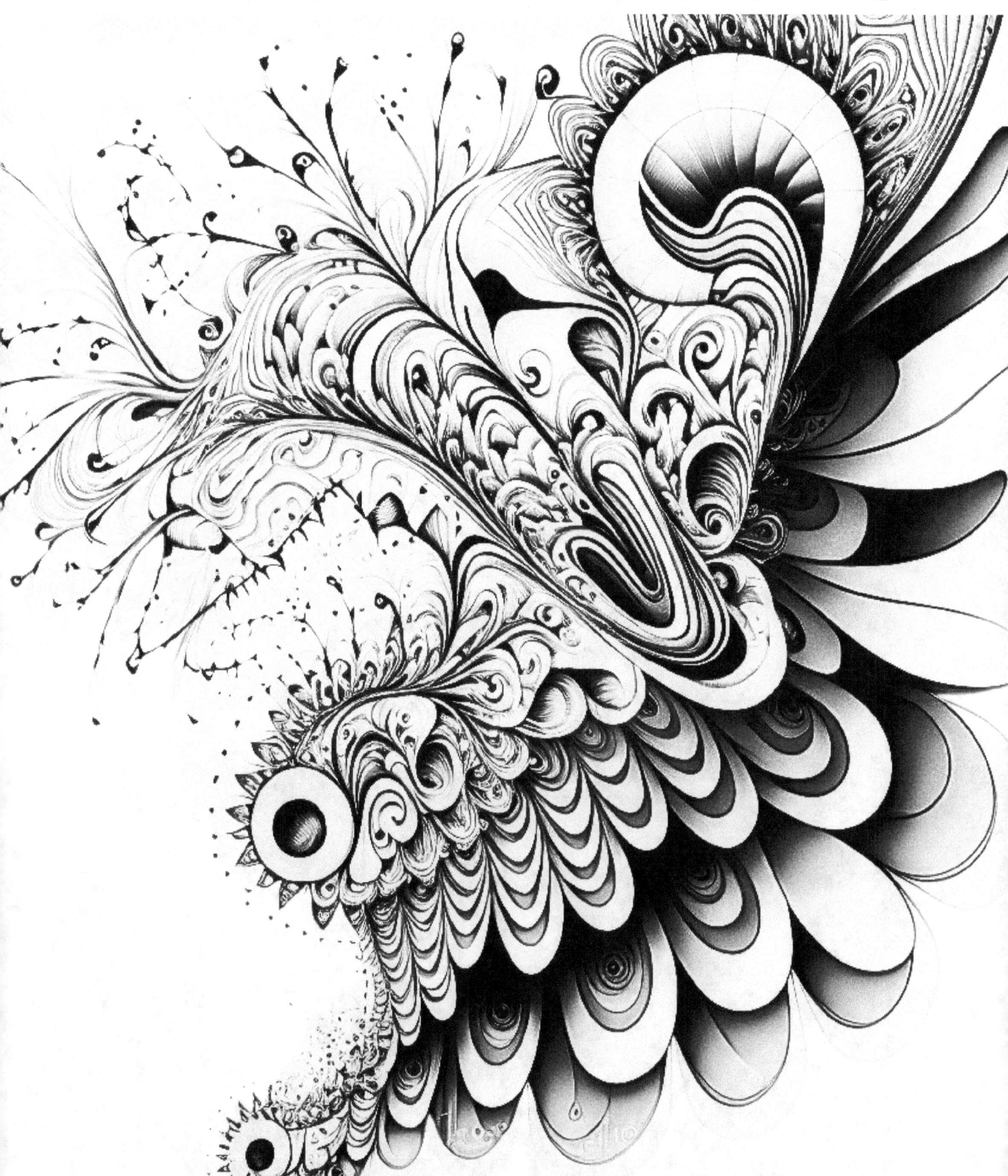

"IF YOU DON'T STAND FOR SOMETHING, YOU'LL FALL
FOR ANYTHING" - **MALCOLM X

FRACTAL MINDS

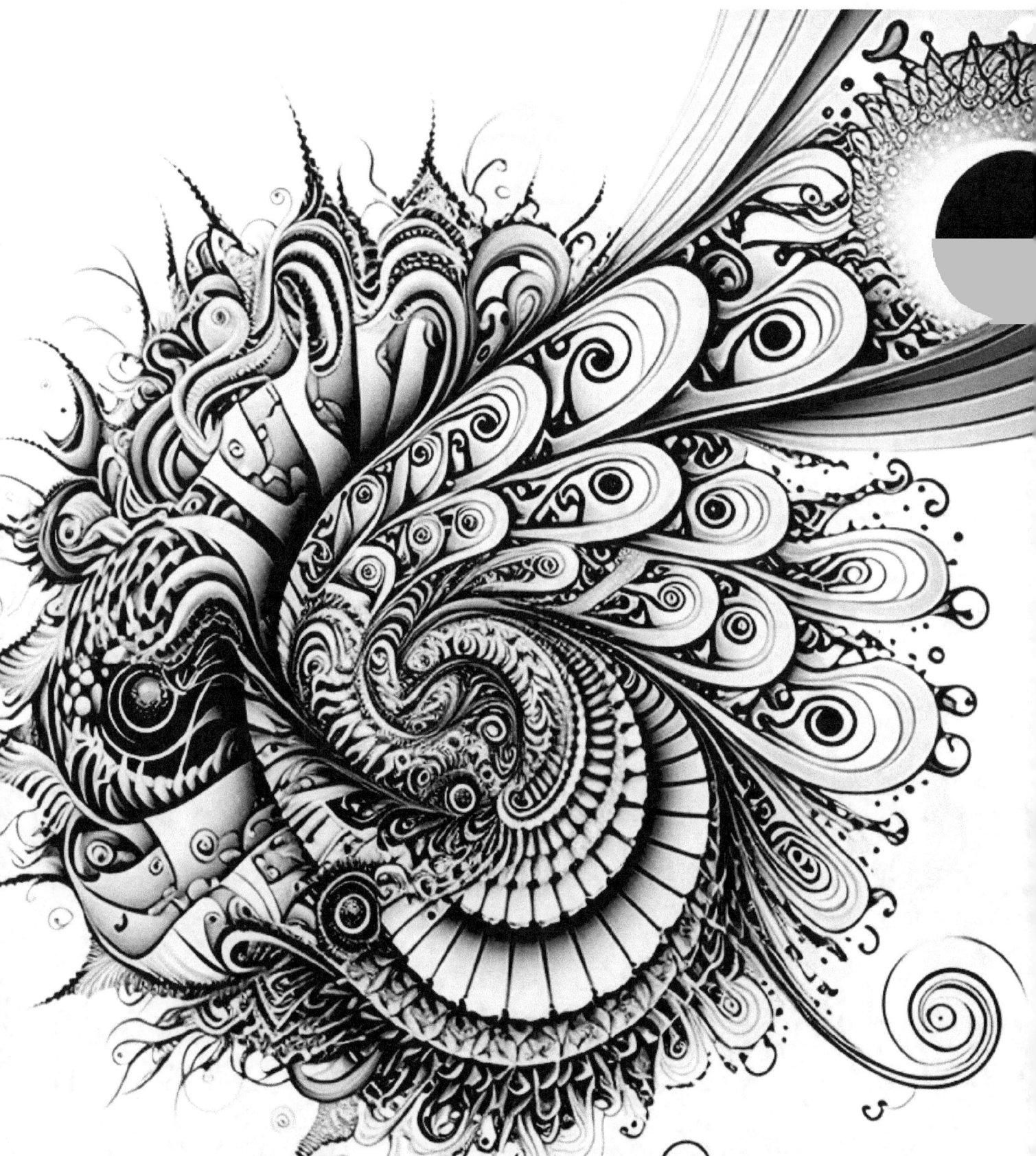

"TAKE INTO ACCOUNT THAT GREAT LOVE AND GREAT ACHIEVEMENTS INVOLVE GREAT RISK." --DALAI LAMA

FRACTAL FOREST

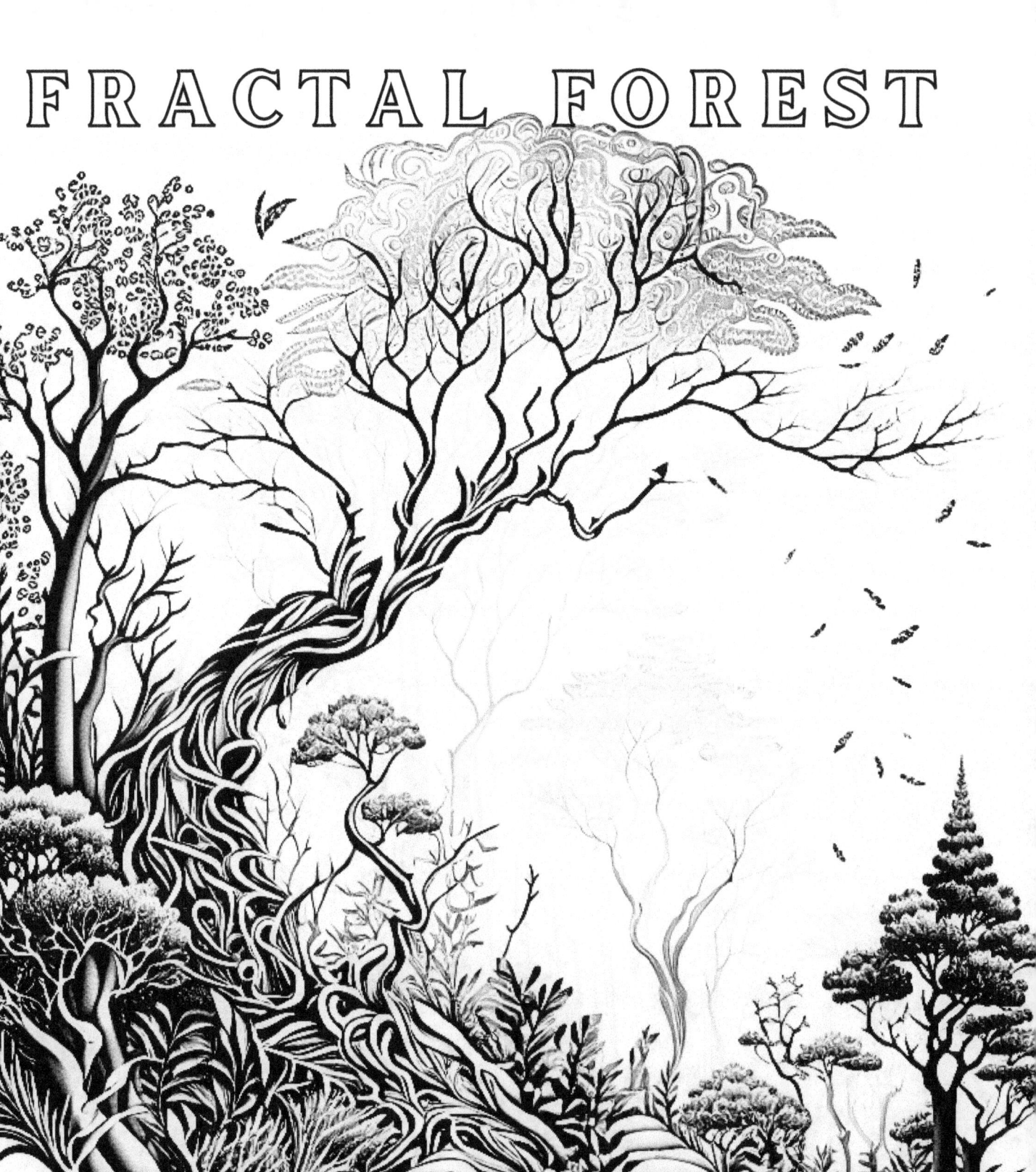

"THERE ARE THREE CONSTANTS IN LIFE...CHANGE, CHOICE AND PRINCIPLES." **STEPHEN COVEY

FRACTAL FOREST

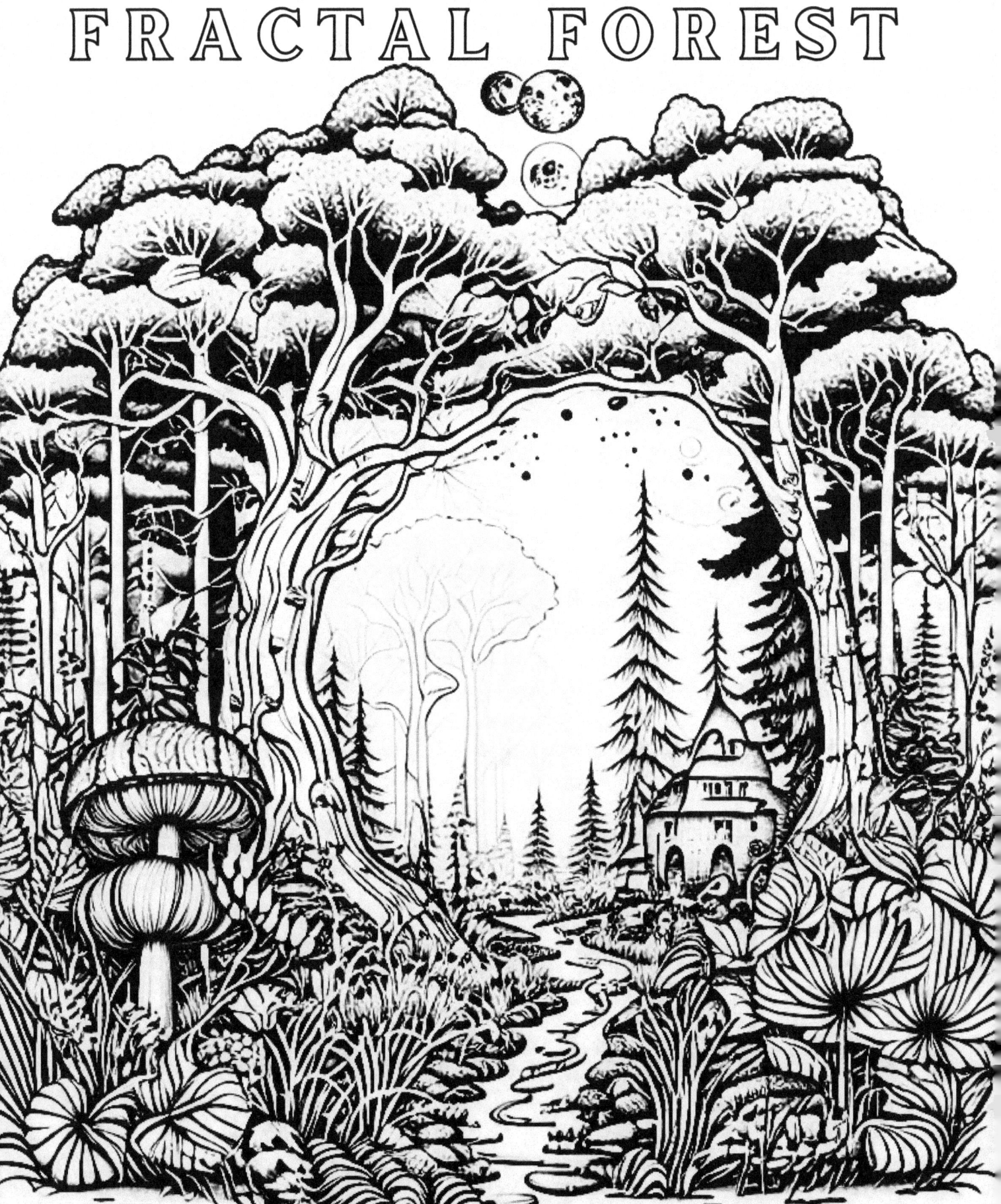

"WE MAKE A LIVING BY WHAT WE GET, BUT WE MAKE A LIFE BY WHAT WE GIVE." --WINSTON CHURCHILL

FRACTAL MANDALAS

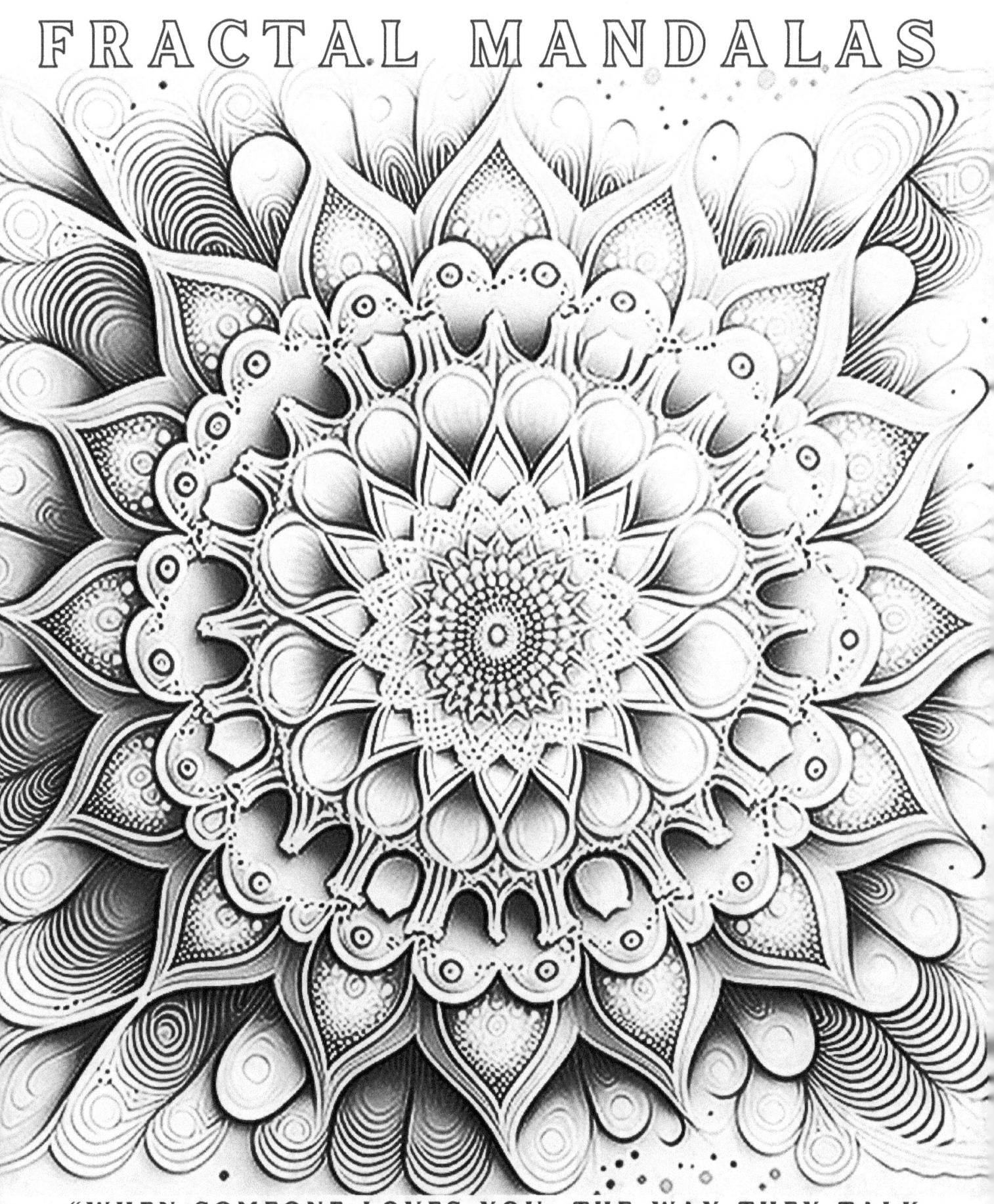

"WHEN SOMEONE LOVES YOU, THE WAY THEY TALK ABOUT YOU IS DIFFERENT. YOU FEEL SAFE AND COMFORTABLE." --JESS C. SCOTT

FRACTAL MANDALAS

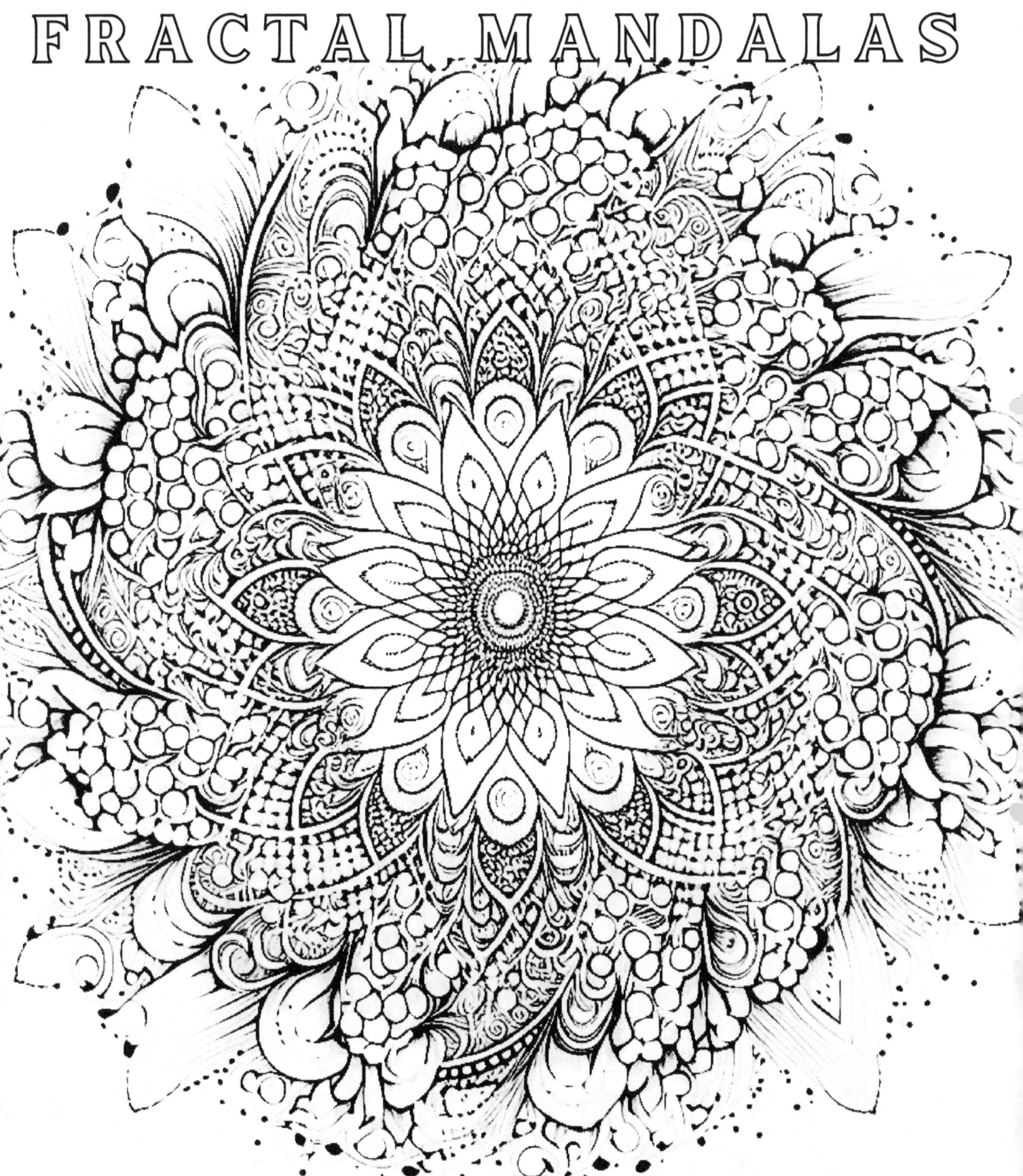

"WHERE THERE'S A WILL, THERE'S A WAY" --SIR THOMAS OVERBURY

FRACTAL MANDALAS

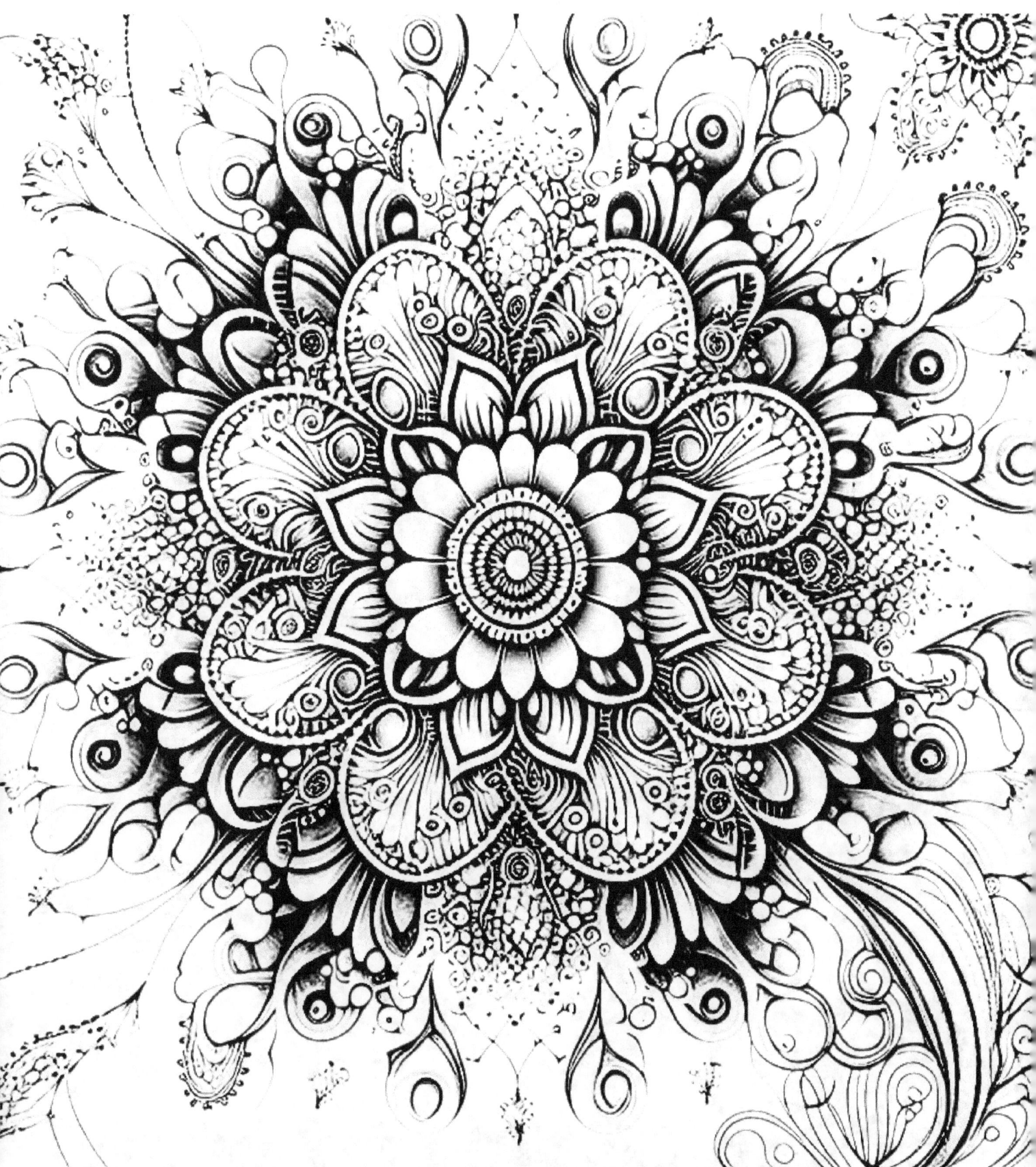

"IF YOU WANT TO GO FAST, GO ALONE. IF YOU WANT TO GO FAR, GO TOGETHER." --AFRICAN PROVERB

FRACTAL HEART

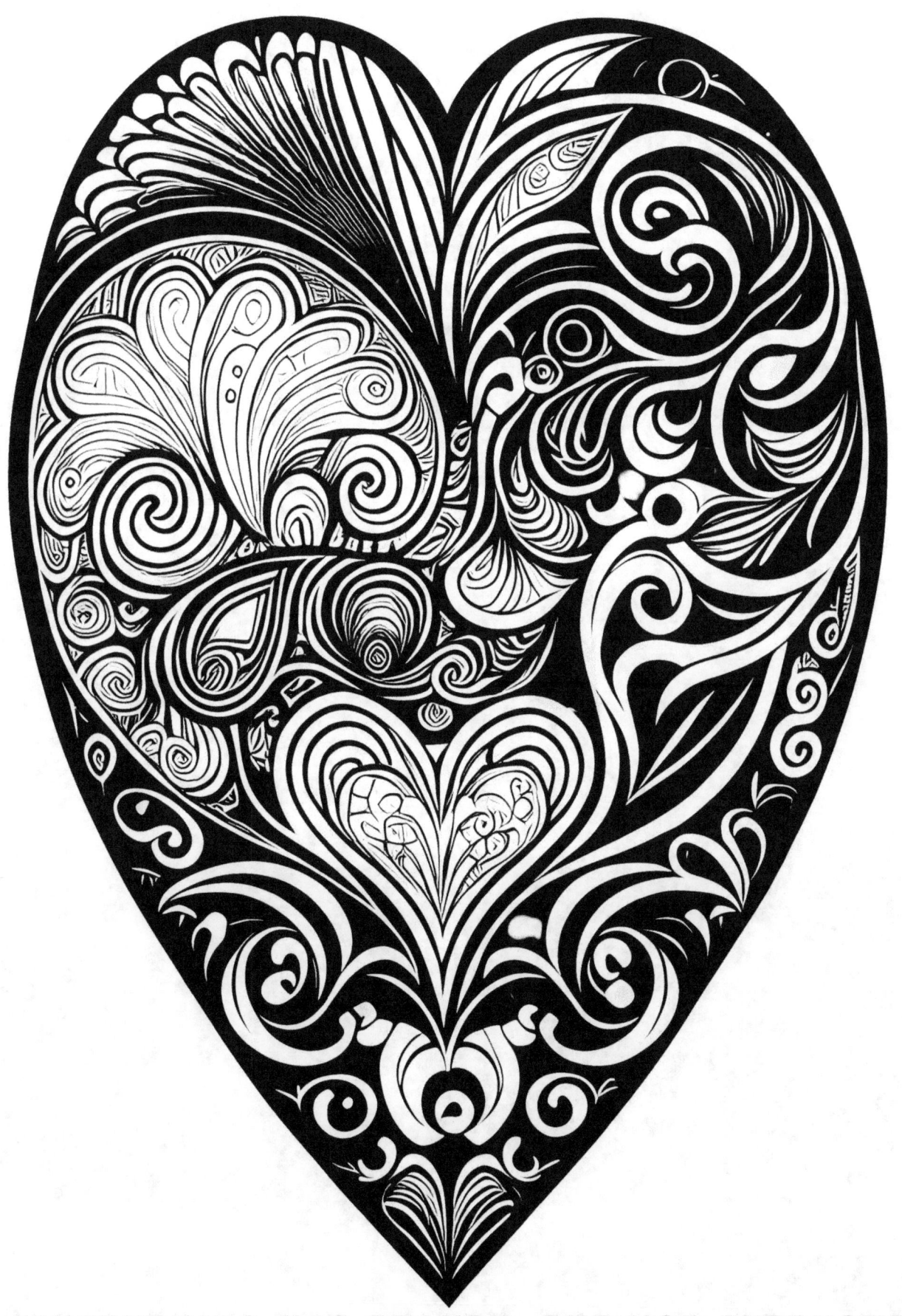

"EVERYTHING HAS BEAUTY, BUT NOT EVERYONE CAN SEE IT" --CONFUCIUS

FRACTAL HEART

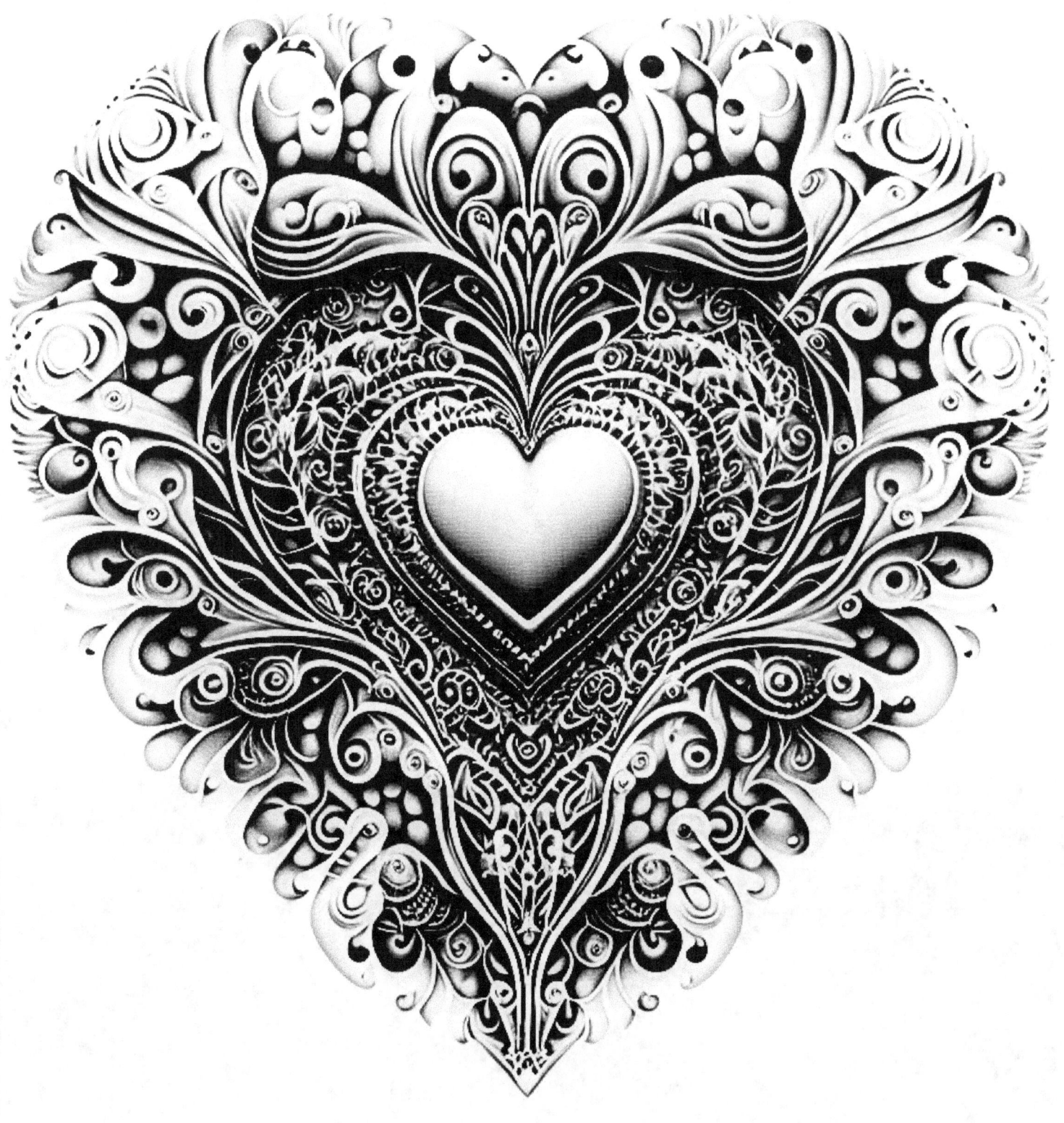

"IF YOU WANT TO MAKE AN APPLE PIE FROM SCRATCH, YOU MUST FIRST CREATE THE UNIVERSE." **CARL SAGAN

FRACTAL HEART

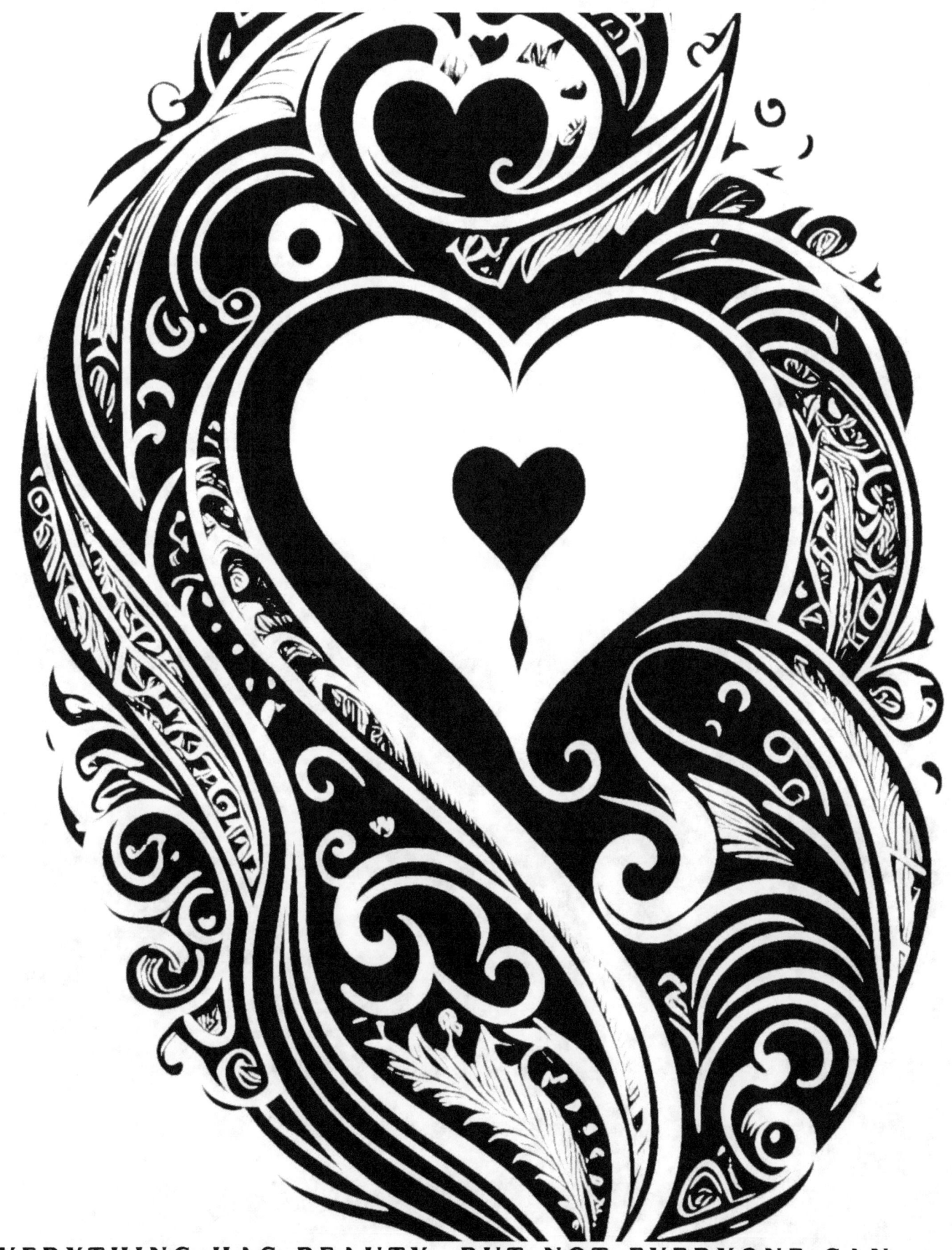

EVERYTHING HAS BEAUTY, BUT NOT EVERYONE CAN
SEE IT" **CONFUCIUS

FRACTAL GODS

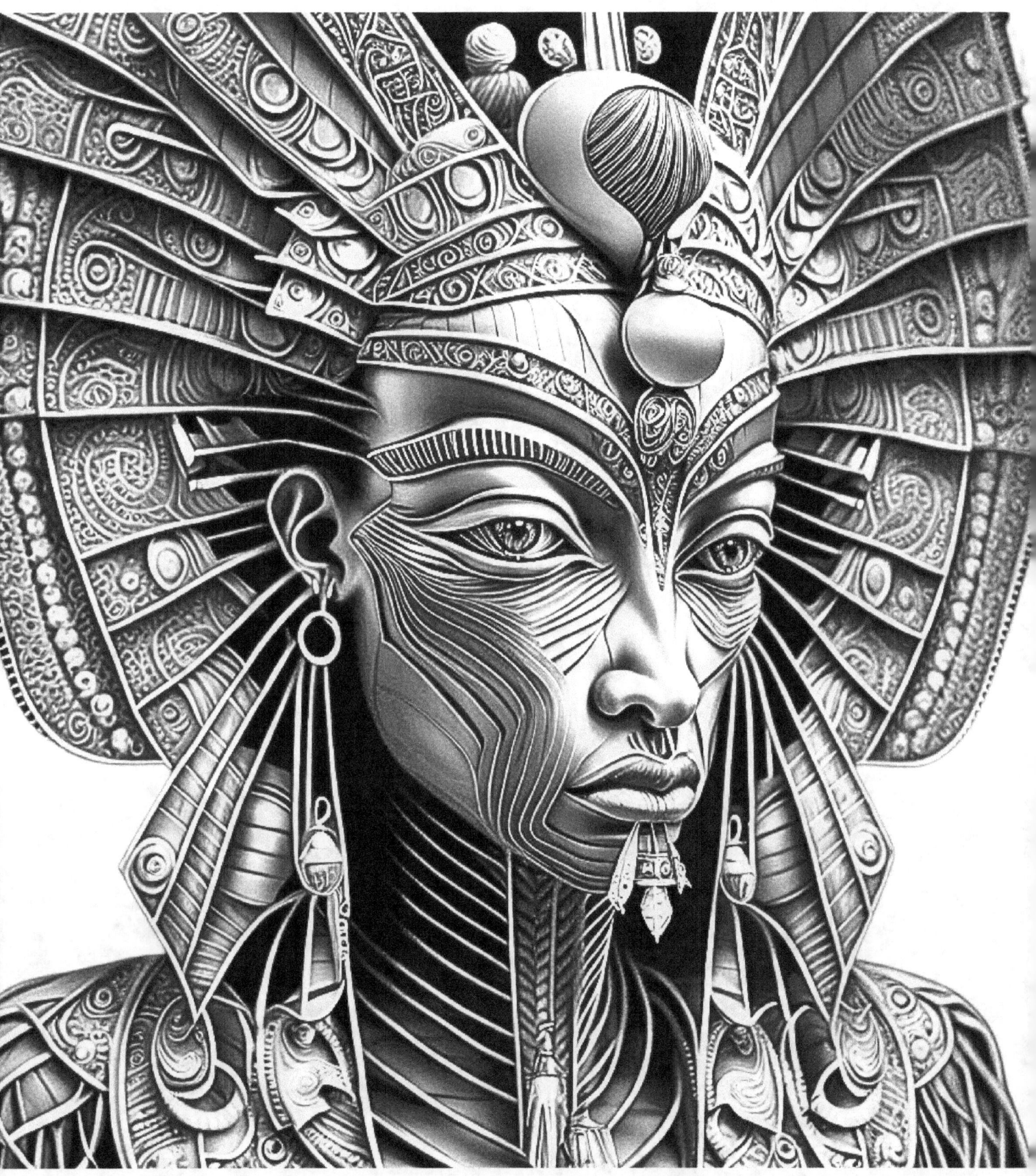

FRACTAL GODS

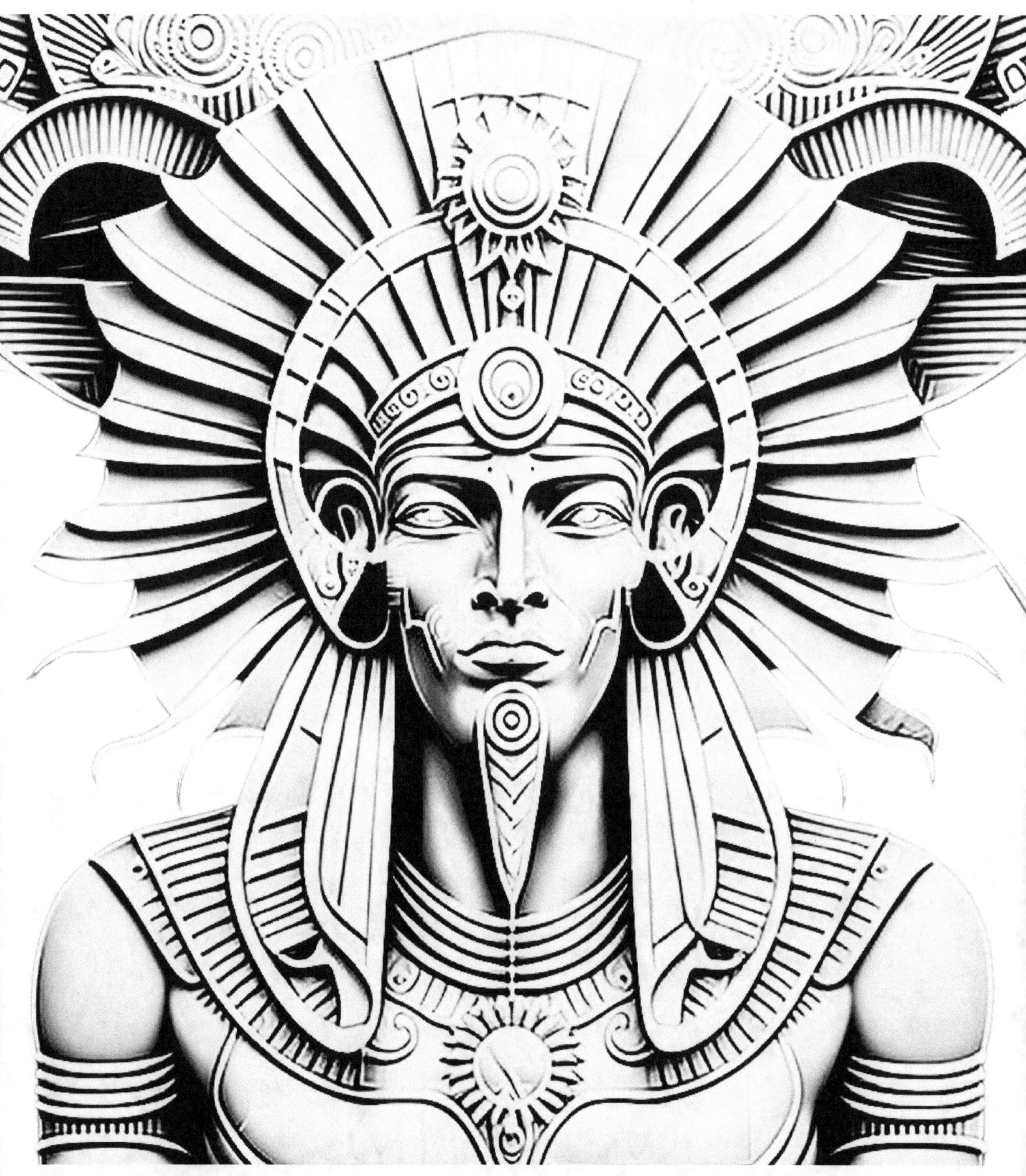

"THE BEST REVENGE IS MASSIVE SUCCESS."
**FRANK SINATRA

FRACTAL GODS

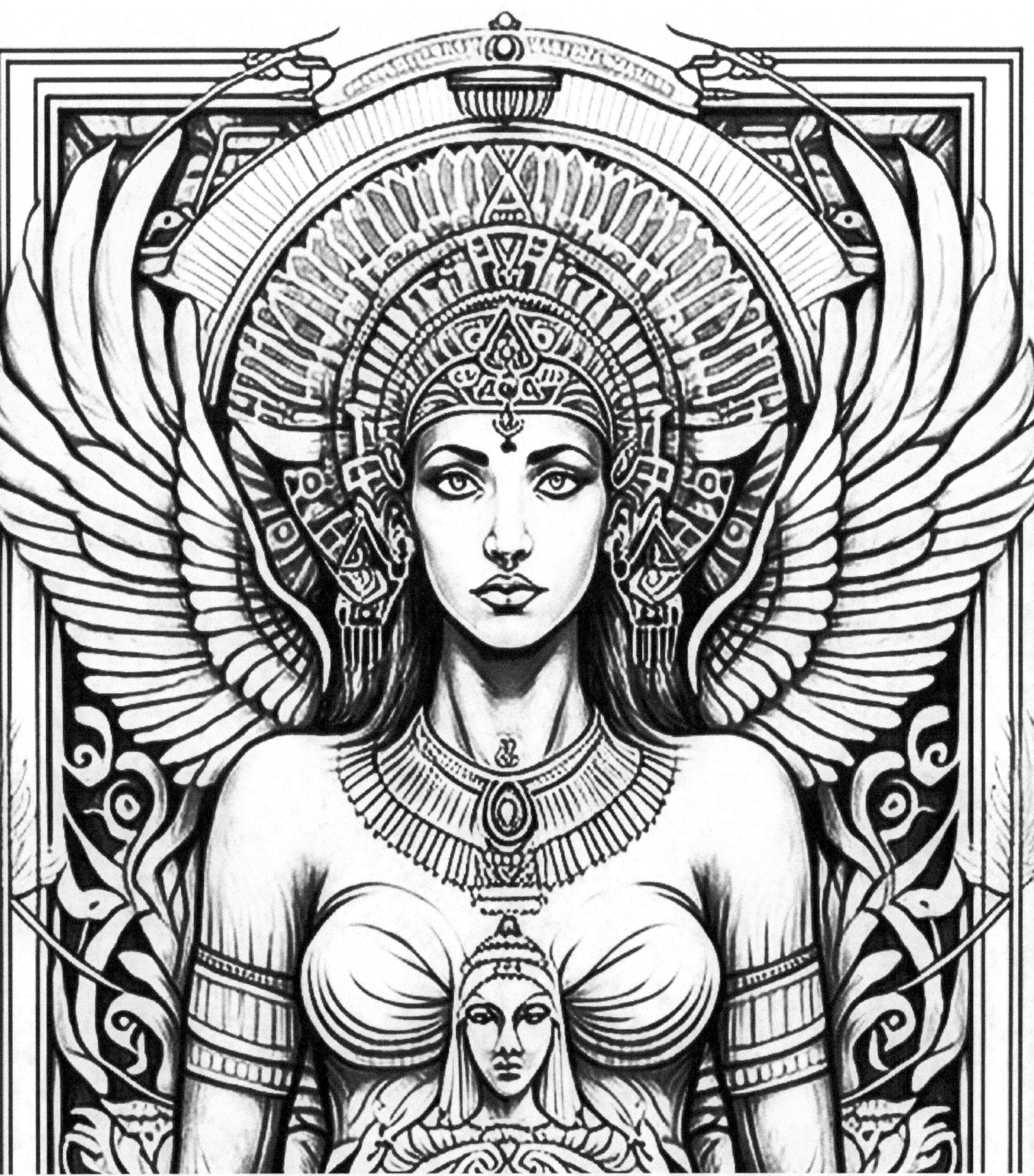

"YOU CAN'T GO BACK AND CHANGE THE BEGINNING, BUT YOU CAN START WHERE YOU ARE AND CHANGE THE ENDING." - C.S LEWIS

FRACTAL GODS

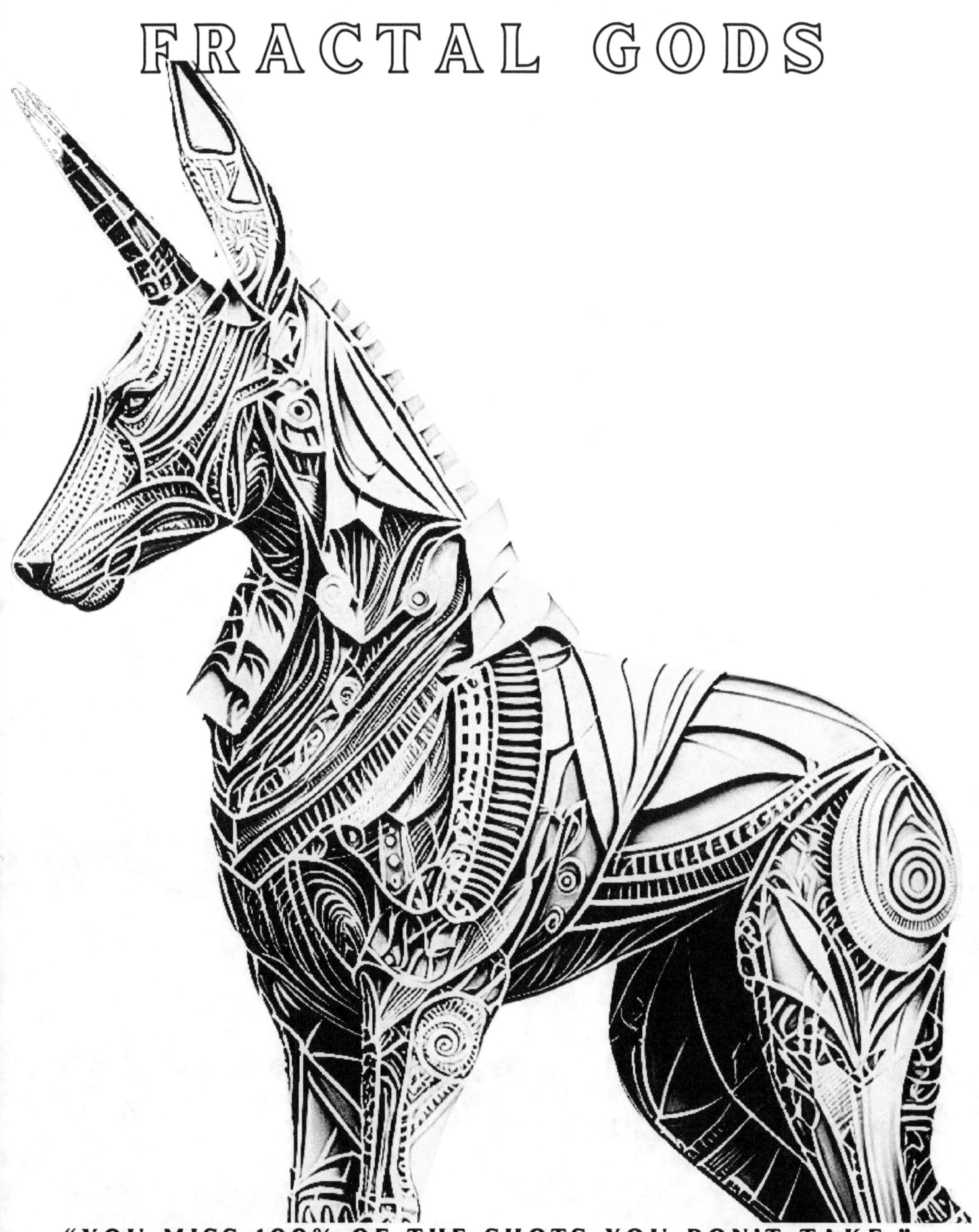

"YOU MISS 100% OF THE SHOTS YOU DON'T TAKE."
**WAYNE GRETZKY

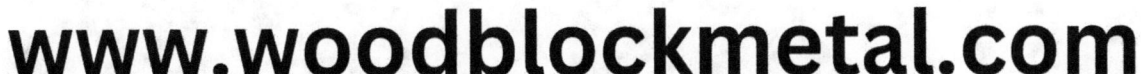

www.woodblockmetal.com